CUSTOM CURRICULUM

N.T. Speedway

Duffy Robbins

Randy Petersen

David C. Cook Publishing Co.
Elgin, Illinois—Weston, Ontario

Custom Curriculum
N.T. Speedway

Published by David C. Cook Publishing Co.
850 North Grove Ave., Elgin, IL 60120
Cable address: DCCOOK
Series creator: John Duckworth
Series editor: Randy Southern
Editor: Randy Southern
Option writers: John Duckworth, Nelson E. Copeland, Jr., and Sue Reck
Designer: Bill Paetzold
Cover illustrator: Jack DesRocher
Inside illustrator: John Hayes
Printed in U.S.A.

ISBN: 0-7814-5155-8

CONTENTS

About the Authors

Randy Petersen is a free-lance writer living in Westville, New Jersey. Formerly the executive editor of *Evangelical Newsletter* and *The Bible Newsletter,* he has also worked with young people and written several books for the youth market, including *O.T. Speedway* in the Custom Curriculum series.

John Duckworth is a writer and illustrator in Carol Stream, Illinois. He has worked with teenagers in youth groups and Sunday school, written several books including *The School Zone* (SonPower) and *Face to Face with Jesus* (in the Custom Curriculum series), and created such youth resources as Hot Topics Youth Electives and Snap Sessions for David C. Cook.

Nelson E. Copeland, Jr., is a nationally known speaker and the author of several youth resources including *Great Games for City Kids* (Youth Specialties) and *A New Agenda for Urban Youth* (Winston-Derek). He is president of the Christian Education Coalition for African-American Leadership (CECAAL), an organization dedicated to reinforcing educational and cultural excellence among urban teenagers. He also serves as youth pastor at the First Baptist Church in Morton, Pennsylvania.

Sue Reck is an editor for Chariot Family Products. She is also a free-lance curriculum writer. She has worked with young people in Sunday school classes, youth groups, and camp settings.

You've Made the Right Choice!

Thanks for choosing **Custom Curriculum!** We think your choice says at least three things about you:

(1) You know your group pretty well, and want your program to fit that group like a glove;

(2) You like having options instead of being boxed in by some far-off curriculum editor;

(3) You have a small mole on your left forearm, exactly two inches below the elbow.

OK, so we were wrong about the mole. But if you like having choices that help you tailor meetings to fit your kids, **Custom Curriculum** *is* the best place to be.

Going through Customs

In this (and every) **Custom Curriculum** volume, you'll find

• five great sessions you can use anytime, in any order.

• reproducible student handouts, at least one per session.

• a truckload of options for adapting the sessions to your group (more about that in a minute).

• a helpful get-you-ready article by a youth expert.

• clip art for making posters, fliers, and other kinds of publicity to get kids to your meetings.

Each **Custom Curriculum** session has three to six steps. No matter how many steps a session has, it's designed to achieve these goals:

• *Getting together.* Using an icebreaker activity, you'll help kids be glad they came to the meeting.

• *Getting thirsty.* Why should kids care about your topic? Why should they care what the Bible has to say about it? You'll want to take a few minutes to earn their interest before you start pouring the "living water."

• *Getting the Word.* By exploring and discussing carefully selected passages, you'll find out what God has to say.

• *Getting the point.* Here's where you'll help kids make the leap from principles to nitty-gritty situations they are likely to face.

• *Getting personal.* What should each group member do as a result of this session? You'll help each person find a specific "next step" response that works for him or her.

Each session is written to last 45 to 60 minutes. But what if you have less time—or more? No problem! **Custom Curriculum** is all about . . . options!

What Are My Options?

Every **Custom Curriculum** session gives you fourteen kinds of options:

• *Extra Action*—for groups that learn better when they're physically moving (instead of just reading, writing, and discussing).

• *Combined Junior High/High School*—to use when you're mixing age levels, and an activity or case study would be too "young" or "old" for part of the group.

• *Small Group*—for adapting activities that would be tough with groups of fewer than eight kids.

• *Large Group*—to alter steps for groups of more than twenty kids.

• *Urban*—for fitting sessions to urban facilities and multiethnic (especially African-American) concerns.

• *Heard It All Before*—for fresh approaches that get past the defenses of kids who are jaded by years in church.

• *Little Bible Background*—to use when most of your kids are strangers to the Bible, or haven't made a Christian commitment.

• *Mostly Guys*—to focus on guys' interests and to substitute activities they might be more enthused about.

• *Mostly Girls*—to address girls' concerns and to substitute activities they might prefer.

• *Extra Fun*—for longer, more "rowdy" youth meetings where the emphasis is on fun.

• *Short Meeting Time*—tips for condensing the session to 30 minutes or so.

• *Fellowship & Worship*—for building deeper relationships or enabling kids to praise God together.

• *Media*—to spice up meetings with video, music, or other popular media.

• *Sixth Grade*—appearing only in junior high/middle school volumes, this option helps you change steps that sixth graders might find hard to understand or relate to.

• *Extra Challenge*—appearing only in high school volumes, this option lets you crank up the voltage for kids who are ready for more Scripture or more demanding personal application.

Each kind of option is offered twice in each session. So in this book, you get *almost 150* ways to tweak the meetings to fit your group!

Customizing a Session

All right, you may be thinking. *With all of these options flying around, how do I put a session together? I don't have a lot of time, you know.*

We know! That's why we've made **Custom Curriculum** as easy to follow as possible. Let's take a look at how you might prepare an actual meeting. You can do that in four easy steps:

(1) *Read the basic session plan.* Start by choosing one or more of the goals listed at the beginning of the session. You have three to pick from: a goal that emphasizes *knowledge,* one that stresses *understanding,* and one that emphasizes *action.* Choose one or more, depending on what *you* want to accomplish. Then read the basic plan to see what will work for you and what might not.

(2) *Choose your options.* You don't *have* to use any options at all; the basic session plan would work well for many groups, and you may want

to stick with it if you have absolutely no time to consider options. But if you want a more perfect fit, check out your choices.

As you read the basic session plan, you'll see small symbols in the margin. Each symbol stands for a different kind of option. When you see a symbol, it means that kind of option is offered for that step. Turn to the options section (which can be found immediately following the Repro Resources for each session), look for the category indicated by the symbol, and you'll see that option explained.

Let's say you have a small group, mostly guys who get bored if they don't keep moving. You'll want to keep an eye out for three kinds of options: Small Group, Mostly Guys, and Extra Action. As you read the basic session, you might spot symbols that tell you there are Small Group options for Step 1 and Step 3—maybe a different way to play a game so that you don't need big teams, and a way to cover several Bible passages when just a few kids are looking them up. Then you see symbols telling you that there are Mostly Guys options for Step 2 and Step 4—perhaps a substitute activity that doesn't require too much self-disclosure, and a case study guys will relate to. Finally you see symbols indicating Extra Action options for Step 2 and Step 3—maybe an active way to get kids' opinions instead of handing out a survey, and a way to act out some verses instead of just looking them up.

After reading the options, you might decide to use four of them. You base your choices on your personal tastes and the traits of your group that you think are most important right now. **Custom Curriculum** offers you more options than you'll need, so you can pick your current favorites and plug others into future meetings if you like.

(3) *Use the checklist.* Once you've picked your options, keep track of them with the simple checklist that appears at the end of each option section (just before the start of the next session plan). This little form gives you a place to write down the materials you'll need too—since they depend on the options you've chosen.

(4) *Get your stuff together.* Gather your materials; photocopy any Repro Resources (reproducible student sheets) you've decided to use. And . . . you're ready!

The Custom Curriculum Challenge

Your kids are fortunate to have you as their leader. You see them not as a bunch of generic teenagers, but as real, live, unique kids. You care whether you really connect with them. That's why you're willing to take a few extra minutes to tailor your meetings to fit.

It's a challenge to work with real, live kids, isn't it? We think you deserve a standing ovation for taking that challenge. And we pray that **Custom Curriculum** helps you shape sessions that shape lives for Jesus Christ and His kingdom.

—The Editors

Five Weeks 'til the End of the World: Racing from the Gospels through Revelation

by Duffy Robbins

Leading a roomful of junior highers through a five-week study of the New Testament is going to be—how shall we describe it?—an *interesting* experience. Working with middle schoolers is always a case study in optimism. After all, here is an age group with an attention span set on "low," hormones set on "high," energy level set on "higher," and whose capacity for talking, laughing, and disrupting is set on "Armageddon."

If you're a little nervous about this, don't worry. That's normal. Even the best youth workers can recall times when they walked into a junior high Sunday School class or youth group thinking they had the gift of teaching, only to discover within a few minutes that none of the kids in the group seemed to have the gift of listening! Believe me, it's in times like these that your "zip through the New Testament" can take an ugly turn. You may find yourself strongly tempted to talk to the kids less about the good news of the Gospels and dwell more on the vivid images of God's judgment in Revelation. (I know I've gotten to this point when I hear myself using Gospel words like "blessed," "rejoice," "love," and "heal" less than I use words like "seven-headed dragon," "sea of fire," "blood," and "wrath.")

Any racing event is going to feature its share of challenges, risks, and excitement. You're likely to find your five-week run on the *N.T. Speedway* to be no different. It won't always be a smooth ride. But, it won't always be "the pits" either. Before we get our engines revved up and shift into the high gear, let's take stock of what we have going for us.

The Shorter the Race, the Greater the Excitement

Only a die-hard race fan can enjoy *every* minute of a stock car race. Let's face it: Who wants to watch a few hundred laps of brightly painted cars driving in circles at high speeds? That's why we have highlight films. In between moments of drama and excitement, a race tends to get a little slow. Two or three minutes of highlight footage are usually enough to capture the few isolated seconds of action in a five-hour race.

Leading a junior high group sometimes presents us with the same kind of challenge: How can I keep my kids interested in a marathon study when they only have a one-lap attention span? Some experts have estimated that the average middle schooler has an attention span of about 40 seconds. (Frankly, that sounds a little high to me.)

Kids simply have little tolerance for names, dates, and details. They want action. They want to keep on the move. Even when they go to a race, it's one trip to the snack bar for every ten laps around the track.

One of the great advantages of taking the "speedway" approach to teaching the New Testament is that it gives us a highlight film of God's work from the Gospels to the Book of Revelation. It allows us to keep pace with an attention span that may be less ready for a "walk through the Bible" and more suited to a "zip through the New Testament." Rather than trying to hack through a ten-week series on Hebrews and Jude that explores themes, sub-themes, and special nuances in the Greek, this curriculum uses more of a "drive-by" approach.

The approach of this series is to zip by and make sure kids see the forest. We'll stop and help them identify the trees on a later trip.

A Race Is More Interesting Than a Lap

People don't go to stock car races to watch any one lap. One individual lap simply doesn't tell much of a story. We want to know how the race turned out. Who ran well? Who lost? Who won? We're more interested in the big picture.

One of the unique features of *N.T. Speedway* is that it allows us to give kids more of a "big picture" view of the New Testament. The idea is that kids will grasp more from our teaching if we help them to get a big view of the whole tapestry of Scripture than they will if we try to get them to appreciate it one thread at a time.

That might be frustrating for some of us, because we'll be aware of so much we're leaving out. But don't allow yourself to get bogged down with detail. A brief look at "who lost and who won" will stay with your kids longer than a lap by lap, blow by blow, in-depth description of every chapter and verse.

Spills and Thrills

In some ways, a "zip through the New Testament" is like any other road trip. The scenery is always more interesting on the first trip. Drivers who travel the route often may forget what it's like for first-time passengers who've never witnessed the sights and sounds of the New Testament landscape.

One of the great advantages of teaching God's Word is the text itself. These ancient, God-breathed pages take us through the eyewitness accounts of the most amazing episode in human history. We read about life, death, romance, hope, failure, and disaster. If we can help kids taste the adventure and human drama on these pages, they will become lifetime visitors to this "N.T. Speedway."

In any other context, we might expect to find stories like these only on the front page of tabloid newspapers. Think about it: "God-Man Demonstrates New Spit Therapy—Heals Many" (Mark 7:32-35; 8:22-25); "Local Teen Falls Out of Window during All-Night Sermon" (Acts 20:7-12); "Man Has Affair with Father's Wife—Church Unmoved" (I Corinthians 5:1-5). Or how about this for a *National Enquirer* headline: "Horseback Hooker Drunk with Blood" (Revelation 17:1-6)?

Don't underestimate the allure of God's Word—even to junior high ears! As you explore the narratives of Jesus, the heart-felt pleas of Paul, and the vivid pictures of Revelation, don't let your own familiarity with these pages sap your sense of wonder and curiosity. If we will allow these pages to come alive with the same color, passion, and urgency that they held for first-century Christians, we may be surprised to discover that "inquiring minds want to know"!

You Never Know What's around the Next Turn

Both the terror and the excitement of the speedway can be traced to the very same fact: You never know what might happen around the next turn. It may be the exhilaration of victory. It may be an unavoidable obstacle. That's what keeps your eyes on the road.

If there is any one predictable characteristic about a junior high group, it's that every junior high group is totally unpredictable! You really never know exactly how kids are going to respond. Sometimes that can be scary; sometimes it can be fun.

The great thing about middle schoolers is that there is still just enough of the "child" in them that they haven't totally lost their sense of play. They haven't been so jaded that they've lost their capacity to marvel. They're still willing to try stuff. If you ask an eighth grader to paint a picture of God using her big toe and the floor of the Sunday school room, she just might start kicking off her shoes!

As you move through this material, don't shy away from encouraging your kids to get involved with the learning activities in each session. Sometimes the activities may seem strange, but go with it. Junior high kids learn best when they're actively involved in the learning process—talking, drawing, roleplaying, writing a rap, etc. Even if your kids seem restrained at first, help them learn that they own the learning process as much as you do. Some of us have been exposed to traditional classrooms for so long, we think that kids aren't learning unless they're sitting still and being quiet. Actually, it's often just the opposite. It's like a race track. When the speedway is quiet, that's because nothing is happening.

Races Are Won by the Crew in the Pit

The best news about this "speedway" is that you have a remarkable crew in your pit. It may seem lonely behind the wheel of that classroom, but don't forget that you are not racing alone. As you lead kids through Scripture, God is at work convincing them that these words are true, that these promises are real, and that they (the kids) need to listen.

Lest we seem unrealistic, we need to recognize that kids don't always respond right away. Don't expect to heat your meeting room with tongues of fire over the heads of your group members. It probably won't happen. You may not even see the fruit of your teaching for weeks, or months, or even years.

Be faithful to keep your eyes on the road, and stay in constant touch with the pit crew. "All Scripture is God-breathed and is useful for teaching, rebuking, correcting and training in righteousness, so that the man of God may be thoroughly equipped for every good work" (II Timothy 3:16, 17).

Duffy Robbins is chairman of the Department of Youth Ministry at Eastern College in St. David's, Pennsylvania. He is also a well-known conference speaker, seminar leader, and author.

The images on these two pages are designed to help you promote this course within your church and community. Feel free to photocopy anything here and adapt it to fit your publicity needs. The stuff on this page could be used as a flier that you send or hand out to kids—or as a bulletin insert. The stuff on the next page could be used to add visual interest to newsletters, calendars, bulletin boards, or other promotions. Be creative and have fun!

Have We Got a Book for You!

Join us as we zip through the New Testament. Buckle up for a wild ride through the Gospels. Prepare yourself for some incredible adventures in Acts. Cruise with us down Romans Road and past the Faith Hall of Fame. Our final destination: Revelation! You'll find all of this and more in a new course called *N.T. Speedway.*

Who:

When:

Where:

Questions? Call:

N. T. Speedway

N. T. Speedway

Meet some of the authors.

You won't believe your eyes!

What does the future have in store?

SESSION 1

Jesus: An Authorized Biography (The Gospels)

YOUR GOALS FOR THIS SESSION:

Choose one or more

- ☐ To help kids become familiar with the Gospel accounts of Jesus' life.
- ☐ To help kids understand why Jesus came.
- ☐ To prepare kids to make a personal decision to follow Jesus and/or spread the Good News about Him.
- ☐ Other ______________________________

Your Bible Base:

Selected passages from Matthew, Mark, Luke, and John

STEP I

Eyewitness News

(Needed: Three group members to perform a roleplay, paper, pencils)

OPTIONS

Before the session, find three group members to perform a brief roleplay. At the beginning of the session, two of the volunteers should pretend to get into a fight—an argument that starts with shouting and escalates into pushing and shoving. After a couple of minutes, the third volunteer should step in to restore peace between the combatants.

After group members have witnessed the scene, have them form four groups. Distribute paper and pencils to each group. The members of each group will have a similar assignment—to present a report on what they just saw. But each group will have a different purpose for its report. Give the following assignments:

Group 1: Your report will be directed toward any newcomers to the group. You will explain who the fighters are and what just went on.

Group 2: Assume that the people who witnessed this fight are angry about it. Explain the fight in a way that will soothe these tensions.

Group 3: Use this confrontation to teach a lesson about how to live.

Group 4: Choose one of the fighters to defend, and describe the scene in a way that makes that person look good.

Give the groups about five minutes to prepare their reports. Then have each group share what it came up with.

Afterward, ask: **Was each report accurate? Did everyone see the same scene? How do you account for the differences in the stories? How did the different purposes affect the way the story was told?**

STEP 2

Four Angles

(Needed: Bibles, copies of Repro Resource 1, pencils)

Explain: **Today we're going to be talking about the Gospels in the New Testament. What are the Gospels?** (They are the first four books of the New Testament. They describe the life and work of Jesus. They are His "biographies.")

What are the names of the four Gospels? (Matthew, Mark, Luke, and John.)

Why do we need four different books—especially when many events are covered in more than one book? Why not have just one Gospel describing the life of Christ? Give group members a few minutes to offer their opinions. If no one mentions it, point out that just as the groups in the earlier exercise had different purposes in preparing their reports, so these writers had different purposes in telling Jesus' story. And, of course, God was using them to convey different aspects of Jesus' ministry.

Ask: **Why do you think God chose these four men to tell the story of His Son?** (All four of them either witnessed the events of Jesus' ministry firsthand or interviewed people who had. The diverse backgrounds of the four men assured that they would write about the events from different perspectives, and would appeal to different audiences.)

Emphasize that the four slightly different accounts do not contradict each other. Instead, they give us a "quadraphonic" report on who Jesus was and what He did.

Have group members reassemble into the teams they formed in Step 1. Distribute copies of "The Gospel Truth" (Repro Resource 1) and pencils to each group. Assign one of the Gospels to each group. Instruct the members of each group to read the "key passages" together and answer the questions.

Give the groups several minutes to work. When everyone is finished, have each group report its findings. As each group reports, the other groups should fill in their own sheets.

Use the following information to supplement the groups' responses.

Matthew

• *Matthew 1:22, 23*—Prophecy was important because it proved that Jesus was no ordinary man. He was the promised Messiah.

• *Matthew 5:17, 18, 21, 22, 27, 28, 38, 39*—Matthew was probably

OPTIONS

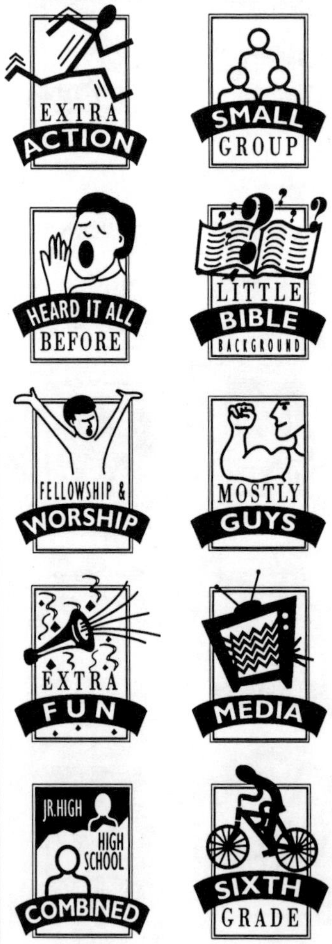

writing for Jewish people, with the purpose of showing Jesus as the promised Messiah and eternal King.

• *Matthew 9:9-13*—Tax collectors were rejected by the religious leaders. It was Jesus who showed compassion for Matthew (who was a tax collector himself) and welcomed him into God's kingdom.

Mark

• *Mark 1–3*—There are at least forty "go" words in the first three chapters of Mark. Some have called this the "Go Gospel." Mark, probably the first of the Gospel writers, wrote the shortest book. He presents "just the facts"—without a lot of sermons or explanations. Jesus' comments in the book are crisp and to the point.

• *Mark 4:35-41*—Mark emphasizes the *power* of Christ—not only in calming the storm, but in healing many people.

• *Mark 8:31-33*—This helps to give us some perspective on Christ. Yes, He was a teacher and a healer—but above all, He was the sacrifice for our sins. This was Christ's main purpose, and Mark keeps that clear. One testimony to the authenticity of the Gospels is the warts-and-all treatment of the disciples, especially Peter. If they were making this stuff up, surely they would have made themselves look better. But it was Christ who deserved all of the glory.

Luke

• *Luke 2:8-14*—Luke was a Gentile himself, and a co-missionary with Paul. He wanted to make it clear that God was offering His salvation to everyone—Jews and non-Jews alike. This was truly good news for the Gentiles.

• *Luke 6:20-26*—The struggling believers would be strengthened by Christ's blessing.

• *Luke 24:36-43*—Jesus actually ate food after His resurrection. Since ghosts can't eat, Jesus could not have been a ghost.

Point out that Luke was a careful historian. Through the years, skeptics have tried to disprove the names, dates, and details in his book, but he always comes out shiningly accurate. Perhaps his scientific training as a doctor was applied to the detail work of researching history.

John

• *John 1:1, 2, 14*—As the Word, Jesus was the full expression of God in human form. Greek philosophers might have enjoyed the first few verses, since they accepted the idea of a Divine Force—but they'd be shocked by verse 14. The Word becoming flesh was a whole new thought.

• *John 3:16*—Jesus is the unique Son of God, sent in the love of God to save humanity.

• *John 20:30, 31*—John wanted to help people believe in Christ. They may have known the facts about him, but now they needed to put their trust in Him.

STEP 3

Mission: Accomplished

(Needed: Bibles, chalkboard and chalk or newsprint and marker)

Choose a group member as an example. Say: **Let's say Nancy** (or whoever) **did something really remarkable. Let's say she ran into a burning orphanage and saved nineteen children. Now we want to tell the world about it, so we're writing a book about Nancy and her amazing deed. What would we put in the book?** Get some ideas from the group, but funnel them into the following four categories. Write the categories on the board as you discuss them.

• ***The Act Itself.*** **We would need to get all of the details of the event—why the orphanage was burning, what Nancy did when she ran inside, and so on.**

• ***Other Things Nancy Did.*** **We might find that this was not an isolated event. Perhaps Nancy regularly showed kindness to children and animals and helped little old ladies across the street.**

• ***Things Nancy Said.*** **In addition to interviewing Nancy about her experience, we might talk to her long-time friends to find out what she was like. We might find that Nancy encouraged others to help people. In other words, she preached what she practiced.**

• ***Nancy's Role in Life—Where She Fit In.*** **We would need to find out how Nancy fits in her society. Is she the president of her class? The homecoming queen? Or is she just an ordinary student? What's special about her?**

After discussing Nancy and her heroic deed, point out that the same four categories can be applied to the Gospel writers' story of Jesus.

Point to the first category on the board. Ask: **What is the "act itself" that the Gospel writers focus on?** (Jesus' death and resurrection.) Explain that over a third of the material in the Gospels deals with the last week of Jesus' ministry. All four Gospel writers include sharp details of Jesus' final days.

Why do you suppose this act is the center of attention in the Gospels? (It's the most important event in human history. Jesus died for our sins so that our relationship with God might be restored. Then He conquered death once and for all through His resurrection.)

Point to the second category on the board. Ask: **What are some**

OPTIONS

LARGE GROUP

MOSTLY GIRLS

SHORT MEETING TIME

URBAN

SIXTH GRADE

of the "other things" Jesus did that are recorded in the Gospels? After group members have given a few answers, ask volunteers to read aloud Matthew 4:23, 24; 8:14-17; and 9:35, 36.

Then ask: **What do you notice about the way Jesus healed people?** (His healings were usually associated with the preaching of "the good news," as if the healings were an outward demonstration of what the good news could do.)

How do these "other things" add to the story of Jesus? (They show us that the crucifixion and resurrection were not isolated examples of Jesus' love and power.)

Point to the third category on the board. Ask: **If you had to boil all of Jesus' teachings—the things He said—down to a few words, what would they be?** Write down some of your group members' suggestions.

Have someone read John 13:34, 35. Ask: **What key word do you find here?** (Love.)

Have someone read Matthew 6:25-27. Ask: **What key idea do you find here?** (Trust in God for our provisions.)

What do the things Jesus said add to His story? (His words give us directions as to how we should live our lives today.)

Point to the fourth category on the board. Ask: **What do the Gospels say about Jesus' role in life—where He fits in the whole scheme of things?** If no one mentions it, point out that the Gospels quote Old Testament prophecy to show that Jesus was the promised Messiah. They also quote Jesus' own words about His identity. He is the only way we can get to God (John 14:6).

What does this information about Jesus' role in life add to His story? (It serves as an affirmation of Jesus' claims. After all, it's one thing to *claim* to be the Messiah; it's quite another thing to fulfill centuries-old prophecies concerning the Messiah.)

STEP 4

What to Do Now?

(Needed: Bibles, copies of Repro Resource 1, pencils)

Explain: **The thing about Jesus is that once we know about Him, we have to deal with Him. We can't put Him on a shelf and say, "Oh, yeah, He was some ancient teacher, blah blah blah."**

He says to us, "I am the Son of God. I died for you. I rose from the dead. What are you going to do about it?" If He's right, we'd better take Him seriously. If not, then He's responsible for the greatest hoax in the history of the world.

Ask kids to turn over one of their Repro Resources and write on the back. In twenty words or less, they should finish the following sentences:

- **Jesus is . . .**
- **During His lifetime, Jesus . . .**
- **Jesus died and rose from the dead because . . .**

For the final sentence, group members may use more than twenty words.

- **If someone asked me about Jesus, I would say . . .**

Give group members an opportunity to finish each statement (especially the last one). Then point out that once we know about Jesus, we shouldn't wait for other people to ask us about Him. We should be *telling* others about Him. Have someone read Matthew 28:18-20.

Before you close the session in prayer, offer to talk privately with anyone who has further questions about Jesus.

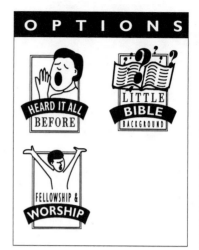

OPTIONS

The Gospel Truth

Matthew

Key Passages

Matthew 1:22, 23

Matthew frequently quoted the Old Testament to show how Jesus fulfilled prophecy. Why would this be important?

Matthew 5:17, 18, 21, 22, 27, 28, 38, 39

Matthew took special care to present how Jesus related to the Old Testament Law and Jewish customs. Who do you think Matthew was writing for?

Matthew 9:9-13

Matthew also showed Jesus' concern for the outcasts of society. Why do you think Matthew would be especially sensitive to this?

Mark

Key Passages

Mark 1–3

Scan the first three chapters of Mark. Count the number of words that relate to "moving"—*came, went, left,* etc. What feeling does this give you about the pace of this book?

Mark 4:35-41

What would you choose as a key word of this story?

What does this say about Jesus?

Mark 8:31-33

Mark didn't build suspense. He made it clear where Jesus was headed—to the cross. Why do you think the cross was so important to Mark?

Most scholars think that Peter was the main source of information behind Mark's Gospel. Why do you think Peter would include information that was so unflattering about himself?

Luke

Key Passages

Luke 2:8-14

Luke is the only Gospel writer to include the shepherds' story. Notice how the angel promises joy for "all the people"—not just the Jews. How do you think the non-Jews in the early church would respond to this? ________________________________

____

Luke 6:20-26

Matthew records Jesus' blessing the poor in spirit. But Luke goes for the money issue—the poor are blessed and the rich are in trouble. How do you think early Christians, bothered by poverty and persecution, would react to this? ________________________________

____

Luke 24:36-43

In Luke's day, some people were suggesting that Jesus didn't really rise from the dead, that He was just a ghost. How does this passage answer those claims? ________________________________

____

John

Key Passages

John 1:1, 2, 14

The word *Word* (in Greek, it's *logos*) can mean "the expression of God" or "the reason for it all." It was a concept that Greek philosophers were toying with, but John applies it to Jesus. How does that help you understand Jesus? ________________________________

____

John 3:16

This verse is more than a sign to hold up at football games. It's a revelation of who Jesus is. In John's Gospel, Jesus is always telling people interesting things about His identity. What does this verse tell you about Jesus?

____

____

John 20:30, 31

John probably wrote his book many years after the other Gospels had been written. People had the facts from Matthew, Mark, and Luke. Now they needed to understand those facts. What does John say his purpose is in writing his book? ________________________________

____

EXTRA ACTION

Step 1

Before the session, put a sheet of poster board at the front of the room, along with a set of finger paints. Make a set of index cards with the names of the paint colors on them (one color per card), and another set with the following body parts on them: thumb, nose, elbow, big toe, little toe, pinky, chin, lips, knuckles, heel (one part per card). Put the color cards and the body part cards in separate stacks. Have kids form two teams. Call out an object or scene that kids must paint. A member of Team #1 has fifteen seconds to choose a card from each stack and use that color and body part to paint as much of the picture as possible. Members of Team #1 will take turns doing this until three minutes have passed. Then give the other team a try, using a fresh sheet of poster board. The team with the most finished picture wins. Afterward, point out that God used four different "human paint-brushes" (the Gospel writers) to give us a picture of Jesus.

Step 2

Announce that you'll give a prize to each team that completes its assignment in six minutes. But each team must complete another task as well. The Matthew group (the tax collectors) must badger the other groups until it gets at least fifty cents. The Mark group (the "action" group) must run through the middle of the other three groups, yelling, "Sorry! Gotta run!" The Luke group (the doctors) must apply a Band-Aid to the forehead of everyone else in the room. The John group (the "big picture" people) must take a Polaroid photo of each of the other groups, waiting for one photo to develop before taking another, and posting the pictures at the front of the room.

SMALL GROUP

Step 1

With a small group, you probably won't have enough people to do the "fake fight" roleplay. Instead, take your group members on a brief walking tour. Don't explain where you're going or what you're going to do. Lead kids out of your meeting area, through various parts of the church, and (weather permitting) around the neighborhood. Whenever you see someone doing something (anything), stop for a few seconds and watch. After about five minutes, return to your meeting area. Then distribute paper and pencils. Instruct each group member to write an account of what he or she saw on the walking tour. After a few minutes, have each person share his or her account. Note any similarities and differences among the accounts. Use this activity to introduce the four different perspectives of the Gospels.

Step 2

Complete Repro Resource 1 as a group. Then have kids form pairs. Assign each pair one of the four Gospels. Also make sure that each pair has a copy of *The NIV Study Bible.* Explain that one person in each pair will assume the role of the writer of the Gospel; the other person will assume the role of a member of the writer's intended audience. (For more information about the Gospel writers and their intended audience, refer kids to the notes in the study Bible that precede each book.) So in one pair, one person will play Matthew; the other will play a Jewish person (Matthew's intended audience). Have each person reflect and report on the information on Repro Resource 1 from the perspective of his or her character. For instance, "Matthew" might explain why he used so many Jewish references in his book. The "Jewish person" may explain what the various Jewish references mean to him or her.

LARGE GROUP

Step 1

Have kids form groups of four. Assign each group the title of a popular movie that many of your kids are likely to have seen. (Use a different movie for each group.) Instruct each member of the group to write a semi-detailed summary of what the movie is about. (The summaries should be no more than a page long.) If a group member hasn't seen his or her assigned movie, he or she must ask someone outside the group who *has* seen the movie to tell him or her what it's about. After a few minutes, have the members of each group read their summaries to each other. Group members should listen for different emphases and information in the various summaries—particularly the summaries written from "second-hand" information. Use this activity to introduce the different perspectives of the four Gospel writers.

Step 3

Rather than using just *one* group member as an example, use several. Have kids form groups of four to six. Instruct each group to choose one of its members to be a "hero." The members of each group should follow the format in the session for "telling the world" about their hero. First, they should decide what specific act their person performed to become a hero. Then they should come up with some other things the hero has done, as well as some things he or she has said. Finally, they should explain what their hero's role in life is. After a few minutes, have each group present its "hero." Afterward, point out that the same four categories can be applied to the Gospel writers' story of Jesus.

Heard It All Before

Step 2
Kids may think they know all about Jesus or the Gospels. Challenge that notion by claiming that a *fifth* Gospel has just been discovered. Kids must tell whether the following "facts" from the new Gospel appear in any of the original four. (All do. See the parenthetical references if kids want proof.) **(1) Jesus had brothers named James, Joseph, Simon, and Judas** (Matthew 13:55). **(2) Jesus had sisters too** (Matthew 13:56). **(3) Jesus said, "I have come to bring fire on the earth"** (Luke 12:49). **(4) One of the disciples was named Levi** (Luke 5:27, 28). **(5) Jesus told a parable about a fish net** (Matthew 13:47). **(6) A prophetess named Anna saw Jesus when He was a child** (Luke 2:36-38). **(7) Jesus said, "The man who walks in the dark does not know where he is going"** (John 12:35). **(8) When Jesus heard that Lazarus had died, He said, "I am glad I was not there"** (John 11:15). Then ask: **Did any of these surprise you? Is it possible that there are still a few facts about Jesus that you might discover in the Gospels?**

Step 4
Christian kids may think that praying to receive Christ is all the response anyone needs to make to Jesus. Help them see past that assumption with the following activity. Bring two or three kinds of refreshments, plus a small pad of paper and a pen. At this point in the session, take kids' "orders" for refreshments (one kind of food per person). Write each order on a sheet from the pad. Then give each person his or her "receipt" instead of food. Use this as an illustration of simply beginning a relationship with Christ—and not going on to enjoy the relationship itself. After making your point, fill the food orders.

Little Bible Background

Step 2
The idea of having four different authors cover (basically) the same story may seem odd to kids with little Bible background. To help illustrate it better, bring in four different newspapers that all cover an area story. Read (or summarize) the story in each newspaper. Then point out that although the papers covered the same story, each paper's article was written from a different "angle" or point of view. The same is true with the four Gospels.

Repro Resource 1 may be difficult for kids who are inexperienced with the Bible. So instead of using it, read aloud a Bible story that appears in all four Gospels. After reading all four accounts of the story, ask: **How similar were these accounts? Why do you suppose that is?** Briefly explain who each of the writers was writing to, as well as some of the distinguishing features of each book.

Step 4
Kids without a lot of Bible knowledge may have a hard time completing the four sentence starters at the end of the session. Instead, read aloud the first two paragraphs of Step 4 as instructed in the session. Then ask: **Why can't we just "put Jesus on a shelf" and write Him off as just a great teacher and a righteous man?** If no one mentions it, point out that if Jesus isn't who He claimed to be, He's either deranged (in which case He can't be a great teacher) or a liar (in which case He can't be a righteous man). Emphasize to your group members that they need to decide whether to believe Jesus or not. If they believe Him, they need to accept Him as Savior and trust Him to guide their lives.

Fellowship & Worship

Step 2
Lead your group members in singing a couple of hymns and/or choruses that deal with Jesus' ministry, works, and life on earth. Among the hymns and choruses you might consider using are "He's Able," "To God Be the Glory," and "When I Survey the Wondrous Cross."

Step 4
After your group members read what Matthew, Mark, Luke, and John wrote about Jesus, give them an opportunity to write about Jesus from their *own* perspective. Create "The Gospel According to __________ (the name of your group)." Ask each group member to write something about Jesus. One person may come up with an anecdote about something Jesus has done in his or her life. Another may write about an attribute of Jesus that means a lot to him or her. Emphasize that kids may write in whatever style they choose—poetry, rap, humorous prose, etc. They may use straightforward narrative, figurative language, analogy, or any other literary device to communicate their message—the more creative, the better. After a few minutes, have each person share what he or she wrote while the rest of the group members encourage him or her with applause, smiles, and heads nodding in agreement. Afterward, you might want to compile group members' writings in a booklet, which you could then photocopy and distribute to your kids.

MOSTLY GIRLS

Step 1

Use a Polaroid camera to help your girls visualize the concept presented in Step 1 a little more concretely. Have them pose for a few fun, crazy shots. Take pictures of the same pose from four different angles. As you look at the photos, talk about how differently the same thing can look from different perspectives—and how seeing something from another point of view gives an overall better idea of the whole. Ask: **Were any of you surprised by some of the pictures and how different they looked from the various angles? Why? What struck you most about the differences?**

Step 3

Say: **So far we've seen Jesus through the eyes of four men. Now let's look at the same four categories through the eyes of one of the women who knew Him best—His mother Mary.** Explain to your girls that because we don't have a gospel written by Mary, much of what they come up with will be speculation based on what they know of her. As a group, brainstorm a list of things you know about Mary (that she was a quiet woman, obedient to God, faithful, loving, loyal, etc.). Then talk about what Mary might have to say about the "Act Itself" (Jesus' life), "Other Things Jesus Did," "Things Jesus Said," and "Jesus' Role in Life." Many of the factual responses will be the same as those previously given, but encourage your girls to try to look at the questions in more of an emotional way, rather than purely factual.

MOSTLY GUYS

Step 1

Prior to the session, videotape about five minutes of a televised sporting event (baseball, football, basketball, soccer, auto racing, golf, etc.). Before you play the tape for your guys, explain that each of them is a reporter covering the event. Assign each reporter a specific "angle" or point of view from which to write about the event. For instance, depending on the sport you tape, you might assign one person the perspective of "Why This Is the Most Boring Sport Ever Invented." You might assign someone else to report on which uniform looks better. You might assign someone else to focus on one particular athlete. After you play the tape, give guys a few minutes to write their pieces. When everyone is finished, have each person present his report. Use this activity to introduce the different perspectives of the four Gospel writers.

Step 2

Ask for several volunteers to act out the story of Jesus' arrest, which is found in all four Gospels. Explain that you will read the story aloud—four different times—while your actors perform the indicated actions. Read each Gospel's account (Matthew 26:36-56; Mark 14:32-51; Luke 22:39-53; John 18:1-11) one at a time. Note the subtle and obvious differences between the passages—as evidenced by your actors' actions. Then point out that the Gospels give us a "quadraphonic" report on who Jesus is and what He's done.

EXTRA FUN

Step 1

Have kids line up. Whisper a nonsense phrase to the person on one end of the line. Have him or her "pass it on," whispering it *only once* to the person next to him or her. When the message reaches the other end of the line, have the last person say it aloud. It's likely that the message will have changed. Ask: **Did everyone hear the same message? How do you explain the difference between how the message started and how it ended up?** Point out that how you hear a message will influence how you pass it along. Such was the case with the Gospel writers. Although none of their messages is inaccurate, each reported information according to how he received it.

Step 2

Before the session, hang a basket from the ceiling so that there's no more than twelve inches between the basket and ceiling. Then tape off a 5' x 5' area below the basket. Have kids form four teams. Give each team a supply of paper. Say: **The object of the game is to get as many paper airplanes in the basket as possible. The only rule is that you may not touch the ground within the taped-off area.** Kids may come up with different methods for getting paper airplanes in the basket. One team might stand outside the taped-off area and throw airplanes at the basket. Another team might slide chairs into the taped-off area and walk across them to *place* their airplanes in the basket. Another team might use the chair maneuver to retrieve the basket and bring it outside the taped-off area. Afterward, point out that different people use different methods to accomplish the same task. The Gospel writers are an example of this. Each of them had a goal to record the story of Jesus. However, each of them used different methods and styles in accomplishing that goal.

Step 1
Show scenes from the following videos (after screening them first yourself).

• *Mutiny on the Bounty*—The first film with this title starred Clark Gable and Charles Laughton; the second starred Marlon Brando and Trevor Howard. Then came *The Bounty* with Mel Gibson and Anthony Hopkins. Show a scene from each in which Fletcher Christian and Captain Bligh disagree. Ask: **How do the portrayals differ from film to film? How might this be like—and unlike—getting pictures of Jesus from the four Gospels?**

• *A Christmas Carol*—Film versions include *A Christmas Carol*, starring Alistair Sim; *Scrooge!* starring Albert Finney; and *The Muppet Christmas Carol*, starring Michael Caine. Show a scene from each in which Scrooge complains about those who celebrate Christmas. Ask: **How do the portrayals of Scrooge differ from film to film? How might this be like—and unlike—getting pictures of Jesus from the four Gospels?**

Step 2
Use a video camera to demonstrate the Gospel writers' points of view with a "Matthew-Cam," a "Mark-Cam," a "Luke-Cam," and a "John-Cam." Have one group member, as Matthew, "shoot" you from an angle that shows you are no ordinary person (perhaps from floor level to make you "tower" over the viewer). "Mark" should keep the camera moving at all times, showing that you're "on the go." "Luke" should stick with close-ups, emphasizing details. "John" should stand far away and zoom in on you, then zoom back to show how you fit into the "big picture." Show the tape as you discuss the viewpoints of the four Gospel writers.

Step 1
Skip Step 1. Before the session, choose a group member who's a good sport; make sure that person will be at your meeting. Decorate your meeting place before the session with signs that honor and congratulate that person (who will be the "Nancy" in Step 3 of the session). When the person arrives, give him or her a homemade crown to wear. Serve refreshments in the person's honor. Let kids speculate about why the person's being spotlighted. Then, skipping Step 2 for now, go directly to Step 3 of the session.

Step 3
Cover Step 3 as written. Then flash back to Step 2, briefly summarizing yourself the distinct approaches of the four Gospels—without using Repro Resource 1 or looking up the passages. Then close with the discussion from Step 4, wrapping up by having kids think about the question, **How can we show that we take Jesus seriously?**

Step 1
Give the opening activity an urban twist. Instead of having kids pretend to get into an argument, ask one volunteer to stand up and announce a breaking news story—a massive fight between two gangs in your area. The volunteer should offer some general details about the fight—how many people were killed or injured, where the fight took place, how much damage was caused, etc. Then have kids form four groups. Give the following assignments:

• **Group #1: Report on the fight from the perspective of the ________** (one of the gangs involved)**, explaining who started it and what happened.**
• **Group #2: Report on the fight from the perspective of the ________** (the other gang involved)**, explaining who started it and what happened.**
• **Group #3: Report on the fight from the perspective of a news team that is very familiar with the two gangs and what's happening in the city.**
• **Group #4: Report on the fight from the perspective of a national news team, one that knows nothing about this area and its gang violence—one that is focusing on the terrible conditions in today's inner cities.**

Step 3
Add an urban slant to the story of "Nancy." Say: **The neighbors in Nancy's public housing building wanted to get rid of a "crackhouse" a block away. So one night some of the people in Nancy's building set fire to the crackhouse—not caring that there were people inside. When Nancy saw the fire, she ran into the building to help lead people out. She rescued a total of nineteen people—most of them junkies—including two of the biggest druglords in the city. None of her neighbors were very happy about Nancy's heroic deed. But we want to write a book about it anyway. What should we put in the book?**

OPTIONS

S E S S I O N   O N E

COMBINED

Step 1

Before the session, arrange to have two of your group members—a high schooler and a junior higher—get into a mock fight. As the session begins, you should be out of the room. The junior higher might start bugging the high schooler by teasing or mocking him and by acting like . . . well, a typical junior higher. Finally, when the high schooler gets fed up, he might push the junior higher down to start the "fight." After allowing the fight to escalate for a few minutes, step into the room and break it up. Then ask some of the "witnesses" what happened. It's likely that your junior highers and high schoolers will have different versions of the story and different opinions about who started the fight. Use this activity to lead in to a discussion of the fact that the Gospel writers wrote about (basically) the same events from four different perspectives.

Step 2

After distributing Repro Resource 1, instruct your junior highers to work together to complete the section on Mark. Your high schoolers should work together to complete the section on Luke. After answering the questions on the Repro Resource, each group should come up with a presentation that demonstrates the emphasis of its book. For instance, junior highers might act out a few stories from Mark in rapid-fire succession, demonstrating the "action" emphasis of the book. High schoolers might act out a couple of passages from Luke that feature Gentiles, demonstrating Luke's emphasis on salvation for everyone. After both groups have performed, go through the sections on Matthew and John (on Repro Resource 1) as a group.

SIXTH GRADE

Step 2

Sixth graders may get bored looking up verse after verse and answering question after question. So instead of using Repro Resource 1, have kids (working in pairs or small groups) choose a popular passage from each of the four Gospels. The members of each pair or small group should read the four passages together and then answer the following questions about each passage: "Who are the main characters in this passage?" "What is going on in this passage?" "What can we learn from this passage?" You might want to write the questions on the board so kids can refer to them as they work. After a few minutes, have each pair or group briefly explain the four passages they chose and answer the questions for each passage.

Step 3

Bring in several juvenile biographies of famous people (Abraham Lincoln, George Washington, Benjamin Franklin, etc.). Have kids form groups. Give each group one of the biographies. Instruct group members to look through the book to find the following information: (1) the one thing the person is most famous for; (2) three other notable things the person did; (3) famous quotes by the person or things he or she said; (4) the person's role in society throughout his or her life. After a few minutes, have each group share its information. Then point out that the Gospel writers used this same kind of "outline" in presenting the life of Jesus.

PLANNING CHECKLIST

Date Used:

Approx. Time

Step 1: Eyewitness News ______
- o Extra Action
- o Small Group
- o Large Group
- o Mostly Girls
- o Mostly Guys
- o Extra Fun
- o Media
- o Short Meeting Time
- o Urban
- o Combined Jr. High/High School

Step 2: Four Angles ______
- o Extra Action
- o Small Group
- o Heard It All Before
- o Little Bible Background
- o Fellowship & Worship
- o Mostly Guys
- o Extra Fun
- o Media
- o Combined Jr. High/High School
- o Sixth Grade

Step 3: Mission: Accomplished ______
- o Large Group
- o Mostly Girls
- o Short Meeting Time
- o Urban
- o Sixth Grade

Step 4: What to Do Now? ______
- o Heard It All Before
- o Little Bible Background
- o Fellowship & Worship

SESSION

2 The Early Believers (Acts)

YOUR GOALS FOR THIS SESSION:

Choose one or more

- ☐ To help kids become familiar with the Book of Acts and the first years of the church.
- ☐ To help kids understand the early church's identity and mission.
- ☐ To encourage kids to be witnesses for Christ.
- ☐ Other ______________________________

Your Bible Base:

Selected passages from Acts

STEP 1

The Initial Activity

(Needed: Post-It™ notes, pencils)

OPTIONS

Choose two group members with different first initials. Give each one a Post-It™ note with his or her initial on it. Then explain: **Rather than choosing up teams to play a game, we're going to play a game that involves nothing but choosing up teams. ________ and ________** (your two group members) **are going to write their initials on Post-It™ notes and give them to as many of you as possible. Once you receive an initial, you are on that person's team. You will then begin writing that initial on Post-It™ notes and giving those notes to others. Once you're on a team, you may not receive an initial from the other team. The winning team is the one that gets the most members.**

It would probably be best for you to hand out the Post-It™ notes when group members request them—but only one at a time. You should also have pencils available on a table or chair somewhere.

After everyone in the group has received a Post-It™ note, tally up the score and declare a winning team. If you have time, you might want to play two or three rounds.

STEP 2

Spreading Like a Wildfire

(Needed: Bibles, a large map of Israel during Jesus' time, copies of Repro Resource 2)

Explain: **Christianity is like the game we just played. It's contagious. Remember the shampoo commercial that said, "You tell two friends about it, and they tell two friends, and so on, and so on"? That's what happens with Christianity.**

For the questions that follow, you'll need a large map of Israel as it was during Jesus' time. You may be able to find such a map in the back of your Bible. If so, copy and enlarge it so that all of your group members will be able to see it.

Have someone read aloud Acts 1:1-8. Then ask: **What does it mean to be a "witness"?** If group members start giving "religious" answers, ask them about being a witness in court or being an eyewitness to a crime or accident. Quite simply, a witness is someone who reports something he or she has seen, heard, or experienced. That's all Jesus was asking the disciples to do—to tell others what they'd seen Him do and heard Him say.

Where were the disciples when Jesus told them this? (Jerusalem.)

Where is the first place they were to be witnesses? (Jerusalem, the city they were in.) Point to Jerusalem on the map.

Where is the second place they were to be witnesses? (Judea.)

Point to Judea on the map. Then ask: **What was Judea?** (It was the region in which Jerusalem was located.) Point out that Jesus was widening the circle in which He wanted the disciples to witness.

Where is the third place they were to be witnesses? (Samaria.)

Point to Samaria on the map. Then ask: **What was Samaria?** (It was the neighboring region to Judea.) Explain that the Jews and Samaritans didn't get along well at all. So Jesus was widening the circle further, both geographically and spiritually.

Where else were the disciples supposed to be witnesses? (The ends of the earth.)

What do you think Jesus meant by that? If no one mentions it, point out that not only was Jesus telling His disciples to take His message every*where,* He was also telling them to take it to every*one*—to the Gentiles as well as the Jews.

How do you think the disciples felt about Jesus' instructions? How would you have felt? (It seems like a tall order for such a small group.)

According to Acts 1:15, how many followers of Jesus were there at this point? (120.)

Distribute a copy of "Palm Sunday to Pentecost: A Wild Ride" (Repro Resource 2) to one of your group members. Have him or her read it aloud as a monologue. When he or she is finished, distribute copies of the sheet to the rest of your group members. As you discuss the material on the sheet, emphasize how sudden all of these events were. After all, there were less than two months between Palm Sunday and Pentecost. Also emphasize how ordinary these disciples were. They weren't superhuman pillars of faith. They probably had just as many doubts and fears as we would have had.

OPTIONS

- EXTRA ACTION
- LARGE GROUP
- HEARD IT ALL BEFORE
- LITTLE BIBLE BACKGROUND
- FELLOWSHIP & WORSHIP
- MOSTLY GIRLS
- MEDIA
- URBAN
- SIXTH GRADE

According to Acts 2:41, how many people were added to the number of believers during Pentecost? (About 3,000.)

After the Day of Pentecost, how do you think the disciples felt about being witnesses "to the ends of the earth"? (They were probably pretty pumped, feeling that anything was possible.)

What made the difference? (The Spirit had worked powerfully through them.)

STEP 3

Who's in the Club?

(Needed: Bibles)

Ask all group members with green eyes to raise their hands. (You may choose some other distinguishing feature—hair color, height, attached earlobes, etc. The point is that you want less than half of your group members in the favored category.) If possible, group all of the green-eyed (or whatever) people into one section of the room.

Say to this group: **Because you have green eyes, you're special. God has showered His blessings on you in a special way. He's revealed Himself to you through Scripture. He's done mighty things on your behalf. For years, you've been told not to associate with brown-eyed people or blue-eyed people because they don't know God the way you do. You've got the idea that they're not good people, that they'll only lead you astray. You should be polite to them if they cross your path. And you may let them watch you worship, but you have a special thing with God that they cannot be a part of.**

But then something revolutionary occurs. Jesus comes to you green eyes and tells you to share His good news with everyone else, regardless of eye color. Everyone can now enjoy God's blessings. The door is open to all who come in faith.

How do you green eyes feel about this? Some may feel like they're not so special anymore. Others may be glad to welcome new people into fellowship with God.

How do the rest of you feel about this? Some may be glad to be welcomed into a relationship with God. Others may be curious and excited about this new opportunity.

Explain: **That's essentially the way it was with the Jews and the non-Jews. Jewish people were specially chosen by God to**

receive His Law and ultimately His Son. But then the time came to throw open the doors for everyone. And it didn't happen easily.

Have group members turn to Acts 10:9-23. Explain that you're going to do an exercise called "Problems and Feelings." In it, you will choose group members at random and ask them to identify with a character in the Bible story. If you ask, "What's the problem?" they have to define the problem facing the character. If you ask, "How do you feel?" they have to explain how the character feels. In either case, group members must respond *as the character in the story*.

Have someone read aloud Acts 10:9-23. Then say to one of your group members: **You're Peter. What's the problem?** (Peter was being asked by God to do something "wrong." At least, Peter had always been taught that eating unclean food was wrong—just as he thought associating with non-Jews was wrong. But things were changing. Now Peter was being told to share the Gospel with Cornelius and his Gentile household.)

Ask another group member: **How do you feel, Peter?** (Horrified? Confused? Trusting?)

Have someone read aloud Acts 11:1-18. Then say to one of your group members: **You're one of the believers who disagrees with Peter in verses 2 and 3. What's the problem?** (The believers had the same problem Peter had. They believed it was wrong to associate with the Gentiles and to eat "unclean" food.)

Say to another group member: **You're Peter in this situation. What's the problem?** (In a sense, Peter was trying to teach old dogs new tricks. God was doing something new here, and the Jewish people were having a hard time keeping up.)

Ask one of your group members: **As one of the disagreeing believers, how do you feel?** (Confused; disappointed in Peter for hanging out with Gentiles and eating unclean food; unwilling to share the Gospel with the Gentiles; etc.)

Ask another group member: **How do you feel in this situation, Peter?** ("Trapped" in the middle between God and the Jewish believers; confused; confident of God's will; etc.)

Have group members look up Acts 15:5-12. Explain: **Paul and Barnabas were off on their first missionary journey. During this journey, many non-Jews were becoming Christians. As a result, a controversy arose. Some of the Jewish believers wanted the new Gentile Christians to follow Jewish customs and laws. The apostles and elders met in Jerusalem to discuss this.** Have someone read the passage aloud.

Then say to one of your group members: **You're one of the Pharisees in verse 5. What's the problem?** (Gentiles were not keeping the Jewish laws. These Pharisees were saying that Gentiles could become Christians, but only if they also became Jews—through circumcision and obeying the Jewish law.)

Say to another group member: **You're Paul in this situation. What's the problem?** (Paul would argue that such restrictions would be "salvation by works." Obeying the law would never make anyone righteous—it just served to point the way to Christ. Gentiles should not be given this additional burden.)

Ask one of your group members: **As one of the Pharisees, how do you feel?** (Angry; afraid that Paul, Barnabas, and the Gentile believers were ruining the church; etc.)

Ask another group member: **How do you feel in this situation, Paul?** (Angry; afraid that the Jewish believers were ruining the church; etc.)

Point out that it was Peter who stood up with the word of wisdom that led to agreement. The final outcome was that the council basically agreed with Paul and Peter—Gentiles are saved by grace, just as Jews are—but asked Gentiles to observe a few Jewish laws for the sake of harmony.

Summarize: **The opening of God's grace to the Gentiles is a major theme of Acts and the whole New Testament. Today many of us tend to "close up" the Gospel to our special group—whether it's racial, cultural, or even denominational. But God is in the business of offering salvation to *all* who will trust Him, regardless of human divisions.**

STEP 4

Paul: Up Close and Personal

(Needed: Bibles, copies of Repro Resource 3, pencils, chalkboard and chalk or newsprint and marker)

Ask: **What do you know about the Apostle Paul?** Write group members' responses on the board. Among other things, they might mention that Paul (then known as Saul) persecuted Christians before his conversion; that his conversion was the result of an encounter with a blinding light from heaven; that he was the "Apostle to the Gentiles"; that he traveled throughout Turkey and Greece, starting churches; and that he wrote several New Testament epistles.

After you've briefly discussed some of the facts of Paul's life, distribute copies of "Paul's Pattern" (Repro Resource 3) and pencils.

Explain: **The last half of the Book of Acts is about the**

Apostle Paul—his journeys through what is now Turkey and Greece, and ultimately his trip to Rome. We don't have time to look at every story, but we can get an idea of a pattern that developed during Paul's journeys. Refer group members to Repro Resource 3 as you go through each point.

- ***Preaching.*** **Usually when Paul entered a new town, he would preach. If there was a synagogue in town, he preached there. If not, he found some other public forum.**
- ***Life Change.*** **Usually, some people who heard Paul preach responded in faith. Jesus then changed their lives.**
- ***Upheaval.*** **As a result of these changed lives, some sort of social upheaval occurs. In Ephesus, for instance, the idolmakers complained that no one was buying their idols anymore.**
- ***Opposition.*** **Because of this upheaval, Paul gained enemies. People tried to kill him, or at least run him out of town.**
- ***Attitude.*** **You might think that Paul got pretty upset about this, but usually he maintained a pretty good attitude. He considered it a privilege to suffer for the cause of Christ.**
- ***Deliverance.*** **God always got Paul out of the jams he faced—sometimes using miraculous means. In one situation, Paul was lowered over a city wall in a basket. In another, Paul's nephew happened to overhear Paul's enemies plotting an ambush.**
- ***Result.*** **Often there was some kind of "happy ending" resulting from Paul's visits. In some instances, people became Christians. In other situations, churches were strengthened. And on all of Paul's journeys, the Gospel of Christ was spread.**

Have kids form groups of four or five. Instruct the groups to look up Acts 16:13-34. Each group should read the passage and fill out Repro Resource 3, briefly describing the events in the text that match up with the categories on the sheet. For now, the groups should ignore the "What about Today?" column.

Give the groups a few minutes to work. When everyone is finished, go through the sheet point by point. In each category, ask for the groups' description of the event from Acts 16. Then ask how that same sort of thing might occur in our lives today. Invite group members to write down their thoughts in the "What about Today?" column. Use the following information to supplement your discussion of the sheet.

Preaching—Paul found where a group of women prayed regularly, and he spoke with them. This is a good example for us today, because it's not "preaching" (which Paul did plenty of), but just talking. We may not be able to preach, but we can talk with our friends whenever we get together with them.

OPTIONS

Life Change—We see two examples of life change at the beginning of this passage. First, Lydia becomes a Christian. Then, the slave girl has a demon cast out of her. How does Christ change people's lives today? Ask for examples that group members have seen—in their own lives or among their friends. Be ready with your own story of life change.

Upheaval—The owners of the slave girl got mad because they had been making money off of her demon. Paul spoiled their business. Christianity can still cause upheaval in people's lives. Some relationships may need to be altered, some habits may need to change. Ask for specific examples of upheaval from your group members, and be ready with an example of your own.

Opposition—The slave owners managed to get Paul and Silas thrown into jail. What kind of opposition can we expect today as we speak out for Christ? Among other things, we might expect a reputation as a "goody two-shoes" in school and some teasing and rejection because of our faith.

Attitude—Paul and Silas sang in prison. Imagine singing hymns after you've just been tortured and thrown into a deep, dank hole in the ground (prisons in those days were not cushy)! What kind of attitude should we maintain as we try to share the Good News of Christ with others? A joyful one—even when people are troubling us.

Deliverance—An earthquake released Paul and Silas from jail, and created a situation in which the jailer came to faith in Christ. Have your group members experienced "crisis" times like that in their own lives? If so, have those times led to unusual opportunities to share their faith? Sometimes it takes a crisis to get people ready to listen.

Result—The Philippian jailer became a Christian, along with his whole family. Invite group members to pinpoint someone they know that they would like to see converted. Ask them to make it a matter of prayer—for courage to share their faith, and for a receptive heart in the hearer.

Summarize: **Christ changes people's lives. As we live for Christ, the people around us will see the change in us. As we talk about Christ, they will respond—some positively, some negatively. Christ causes upheaval, and some people don't want to be bothered. It's interesting that the enemies of Paul and Silas once called them "these men who have caused trouble all over the world"** (Acts 17:6)**. That's the way some people will think of us. But others will thank us for being true to the Gospel.**

STEP 5

Can I Get a Witness?

In closing, remind group members of Jesus' words in Acts 1:8: "You will be my witnesses." Explain that we don't need to be great preachers like Paul, but we should be able to tell others about Christ, as we've experienced Him in our lives.

Ask each group member to identify one thing that he or she could do this week to be a "witness" for Christ. Maybe it's talking to someone. Maybe it's making a hard (but right) decision. Maybe it's being friendly to the class outcast. Maybe it's just spending an hour in prayer, asking God to open his or her eyes to people's needs. Whatever it is, it should be specific and do-able *this week*. Instruct group members to write their ideas at the bottom of Repro Resource 3.

Close the session in prayer, asking God for courage and wisdom for your group members as they follow through on their ideas.

OPTIONS

FELLOWSHIP & WORSHIP

MOSTLY GUYS

EXTRA FUN

JR. HIGH HIGH SCHOOL COMBINED

Palm Sunday to Pentecost: A Wild Ride

It was a strange time for all of us. It's hard to believe it was less than two months ago that Jesus decided to go to Jerusalem for Passover. We knew there was danger there, but we couldn't talk Him out of it. When He entered the city on that glorious Sunday, we thought maybe things were going to be all right.

But as we sat in our borrowed dining room that Thursday, sharing the Passover meal, things began to go wrong. Judas left the table suddenly. Later, he brought the temple guards to our secret hideout on the Mount of Olives. They arrested Jesus, and took Him to trial. He was convicted, tortured, and crucified. All of this happened within twenty-four hours.

Most of us feared for our lives, lying low in the city until we could safely escape back to Galilee. But on Sunday we heard the most remarkable news. Jesus was alive again! We vaguely remembered that He had predicted this, but we had never expected such a great miracle. We gathered back in our upper room, and there the risen Jesus appeared to us.

The next forty days were a whirlwind of activity. Jesus was with us sometimes, and sometimes not. He would meet with us like before. But He was teaching us more intently now. I guess He had always tried to teach us, but now we were ready to learn. He taught us what the Scriptures said about Him—about His death and resurrection. He told us to spread this truth about Him, to tell others what we had experienced—not just in Judea, but all over the world!

Shortly before He left us, He told us to stay in Jerusalem. He said He was going to give us a special gift—a special power—but we would have to wait for it. Then, as He was talking one day, He ascended into heaven. We saw angels welcoming Him with great joy. But we were left without our Lord. We could only wait for that special power.

A week went by. We camped out in that same room, praying together. We even selected a replacement for Judas. A few more days went by. The Day of Pentecost arrived, when Jews from all over the world returned to Jerusalem. And then it happened. All heaven broke loose.

We suddenly found ourselves speaking languages we didn't understand. There was a power within us that we had never felt before. It was as if Jesus was with us again. We ran out to the temple area, where people were gathering from all around the world. We spoke in these strange languages, and they listened. On that day alone, 3,000 people decided to follow Jesus. And that was just the beginning.

PAUL'S PATTERN

Event	Acts 16	What about Today?
Preaching		
Life change		
Upheaval		
Opposition		
Attitude		
Deliverance		
Result		

One thing I could do this week to be a witness for Christ is . . .

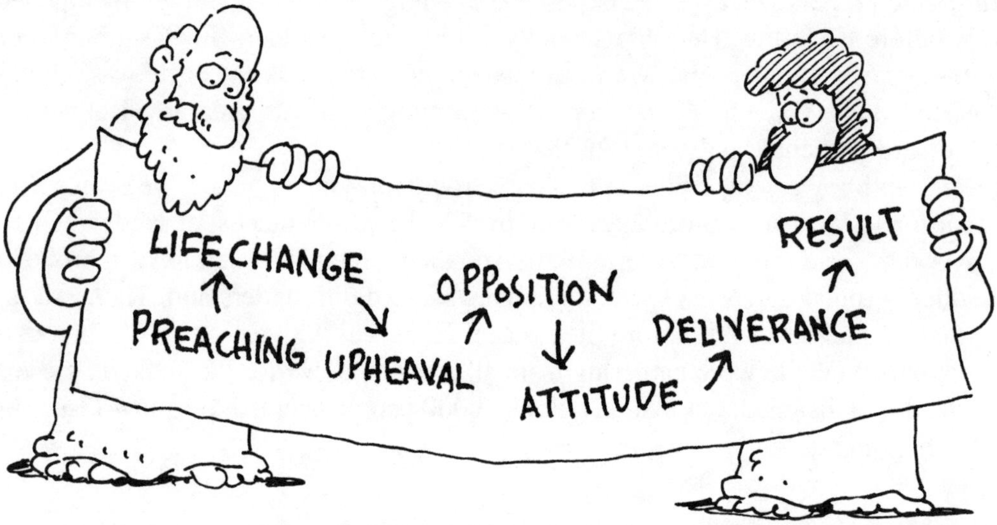

EXTRA ACTION

Step 2
Instead of just reading Repro Resource 2, have kids perform the actions of the disciples as you're reading. But to echo the "wild ride" emphasis, have them act in fast motion, speeded up. To add to the old silent-movie feel, you might want to play a rinky-tink piano recording (such as a selection from Marvin Hamlisch's album *The Entertainer*) and even aim a strobe light at the actors. If you like, award a prize for the speediest performance.

Step 3
After the green-eyed exercise, try another activity. Have kids stand in a circle, close together. Instruct each person to tape a paper plate to the floor under his or her feet. Using a wide, permanent marker, write a *P* on one plate and an *F* on another. As you read the first Acts passage, have kids walk in a circle, listening. When you stop reading, the person standing on the *P* plate must answer your "What's the problem?" question; the person standing on the *F* plate must answer your "How do you feel?" question. Repeat the process with each passage.

SMALL GROUP

Step 1
Since the Post-it™ activity probably would take less than ten seconds with a small group, have your kids play "Multiple-It Tag" instead. Choose one person to be "It." Have him or her stand in the middle of the room. Explain that he or she may move only two steps (in any direction) from where he or she is standing. Instruct the rest of the kids to stand at one end of the room. When you give the signal. they will try to cross to the other side without being tagged by "It." Those who are tagged will also become "It." For the next round, they will also stand in the middle of the room, trying to tag the rest of the group members (who are trying to cross to the other side of the room again). Continue playing until you have one "non-It" remaining. [NOTE: If you have only a small space available, try having kids play the game blindfolded.]

Step 4
Before you start your discussion of Paul, have each group member write down one thing he or she knows about the apostle—something that might be mentioned in the upcoming discussion of Paul. Then work on Repro Resource 3 as a group. As you go through the discussion of Paul's life in the session, if you mention something that a group member wrote down, he or she should stand (and remain standing for the rest of the discussion). At the end of the discussion, award prizes to those who are standing for being such insightful forecasters. Then ask the rest of the kids to share what they wrote, perhaps filling in some "gaps" in your discussion.

LARGE GROUP

Step 2
Note that the size of your group may be comparable to the size of the total body of believers after Jesus' death. Have someone read aloud Acts 2:41, which tells us that at Pentecost, approximately three thousand people became believers. Emphasize that Pentecost occurred less than two months after Jesus' death. That's church growth! Suggest to your kids that they have the same potential for spreading the Gospel that the first-century Christians did. Instruct each group member to write down the names of six non-Christians that he or she could share the Gospel with. Assume that of those six people, three become Christians and share their new faith with six other people. Continue working out the equation until you reach a total of three thousand new Christians. As you wrap up the session in Step 5, encourage kids to get started on this project by sharing their faith with the six people on their list.

Step 3
Before the session, create a list of twenty characteristics ("Has never flown in an airplane," "Wears larger than a size 12 shoe," "Was born in September," etc.) Make copies of the list for your kids. At this point in the session, pass out the lists. Give kids about five minutes to find out how many characteristics apply to other group members. The easiest way to do this is to have kids sign their names by characteristics that apply to them. Afterward, ask: **What if the only people who were eligible to become Christians were people who fit one of these characteristics? How would the rest of you feel?** Point out that this is similar to the situation in the early church. Originally, only Jewish people were chosen to receive God's Son. So it was a radical change when Peter and Paul preached that salvation was available to both Jews and Gentiles.

Heard It All Before

Step 2
Kids may know but not care about the early church. Play a recording of Billy Joel's song "We Didn't Start the Fire," which condenses several decades of American history. Ask: **What does the title of the song mean? Who "started the fire" where the church is concerned? Why bother to learn what's happened in our nation's history? How could knowing how the church's "fire" started help us today?** As needed, point out that (1) we need to know where we've been to know where we're going; (2) we need to know what worked in the past so that we can adapt it for today; and (3) we need to know what didn't work so that we can avoid past mistakes.

Step 4
Kids may have gotten the idea that Paul was dull and emotionless, not quite human—making him hard to get enthusiastic about. You may want to look at passages like these, in which Paul reveals very human feelings: Romans 7:21-24 (frustration over his sins); Romans 8:26 (inability to express himself); Galatians 3:1; 5:2, 12 (anger, earthy language); II Timothy 4:9-13 (loneliness and need for physical comfort). In Step 5, you may need a fresh approach to get past kids' defenses concerning witnessing. Ask them to make a list of people they know who *don't deserve* to go to heaven. Some may have trouble coming up with names; others may want to include everyone, saying that no one really deserves to go to heaven. Then ask kids to list people they know who don't deserve to know *how* to get to heaven. Chances are these lists will be short or nonexistent. Encourage kids to consider the implication—that everyone they know deserves to hear the Good News. Ask: **How will they hear it, if not from you?**

Little Bible Background

Step 2
Kids with little Bible background may tune out your discussion of Jerusalem, Judea, Samaria, and the ends of the earth. To keep their interest, you might want to use a simple demonstration of how the Gospel should be spread. After discussing what a "witness" is, lead your group members outside. Try to find a dandelion (the kind with the white fluffy spores—not the yellow ones). Blow on the top of the dandelion. As the white spores are carried away by the wind, explain that when they land, their seeds will cause new plants to grow. Point out that this is like being witnesses. The people we witness to will carry the Gospel message to other areas of the world, guaranteeing that the message will continue to spread.

Step 3
To kids without much Bible background, the fact that Jewish people were specially chosen by God to receive His Son may seem like discrimination against Gentiles (anyone who is not Jewish). Have someone read aloud Romans 1:16. Point out that the Jews weren't offered the Gospel *exclusively*; they were offered it *first*. It was then their responsibility to carry that Gospel to other people (including Gentiles). To summarize the issue of who may receive salvation, have someone read aloud Romans 10:12.

Fellowship & Worship

Step 2
Lead your group members in singing a couple of hymns and/or choruses that deal with being "witnesses" for Christ. Among the hymns you might consider using is "O For a Thousand Tongues to Sing."

Step 5
Have kids form pairs. Instruct each person to tell his or her partner about a non-Christian he or she knows. In addition to describing the person, group members should also describe for their partners their relationship with the person. For instance, someone might say, "One of my best friends is a non-Christian. We get along really well, and enjoy the same things. He knows I'm a Christian, but he doesn't say much about it—except sometimes he calls me 'Churchboy.'" After hearing about the person's relationship with the non-Christian, his or her partner should offer some suggestions on how the person might be a "witness" to the non-Christian. For example, the partner of the person in the earlier example might say, "If you and your friend enjoy the same things, try to convince him that he might enjoy coming to church or youth group with you—if he gives it a chance." Encourage the partners to check in with each other during the week to see how their "witnessing" is going.

MOSTLY GIRLS

Step 2

Ask your girls to think of the latest fad—fashion or otherwise—to hit their school. Ask: **How did you find out about it? How quickly did it spread? How soon did everyone catch on?** Use this example to help them see that when we're excited about something and really like it, we're anxious to tell others. News of it spreads quickly. Then ask: **What were some fads you can think of that came and went within the last year?** Your girls should be able to think of a least a few short-lived fads. Point out that Christianity had its start in much the same way as these fads. People were excited about it and wanted to tell others—although Christianity is not a fad and will not fade away.

Step 3

To help group members understand how difficult it must have been for the Jews to hear that they were to spread the Gospel to the Samaritans, ask your girls to place themselves in the following situation, and then talk about how they would feel. Say: **Your school just got a new principal who is on a goodwill kick. She comes to each class personally to leave each of you with a challenge. She'd like to wipe out cliques, gangs, and the social order that has reigned in your school for ages. She challenges each of you to sit with someone new at lunch a couple times a week, and make a new friend in each of your classes. She even wants to end the crosstown rivalry with another school by organizing a combined dance. The rivalries and "class structures" are strong and have existed for years, and you've worked your way to the top. To start reaching out to others would mean you would lose your status. What are you going to do? Why?**

MOSTLY GUYS

Step 3

Instead of using "green eyes" as a distinguishing feature for the activity at the beginning of the step, use a categorization guys are more likely to have faced. Ask all of the guys who are on a sports team at school to stand up. If this category includes less than half of your group, use this as the distinguishing feature. If not, narrow the field some more by having everyone who isn't on a *particular* sports team (basketball, baseball, football, tennis, etc.) sit down. Explain that those who are left standing are special in God's eyes. He's showered all kinds of blessings on them. They've been told not to associate with people who aren't involved in their sport, lest they lose their "competitive edge." Continue the discussion, following the instructions in the session, but making changes as necessary for this new categorization.

Step 5

Wrap up the session by talking to your guys about being "witnesses" for Christ (Acts 1:8). Point out that our actions and the way we treat people are as much a part of being a witness as talking to people about Christ. As a group, discuss some specific ways your guys can be witnesses for Christ through their actions. Suggestions might include things like not cutting on classmates when you're hanging out with the guys, treating non-jocks as kindly as you would your athletic buddies, making a point to be sincere to some members of the opposite sex, etc. Ask each of your group members to consider becoming an "accountability partner" with someone else in the group, occasionally asking each other if their actions are contributing to their "witness" for Christ.

EXTRA FUN

Step 3

Explain that you're going to throw a party in your meeting area. (You'll need snacks and drinks.) Instruct kids to leave the room. Explain that they may re-enter (and attend the party) only if they meet a certain qualification. However, only you know what that qualification is. (Perhaps you might allow only kids who are wearing a certain brand of tennis shoe to enter.) Have kids come to the door one at a time. Pretend to look them over, as if you're judging whether they're worthy to attend. Allow kids who meet the qualification to enter. Then start the party by breaking out the food and turning on some music. Meanwhile, those who weren't allowed to enter will be wondering why they were excluded. After a few minutes, stop the party and invite the rest of the kids in. Reveal what the qualification was. Then explain that originally, to be qualified to receive God's special blessings, a person had to be Jewish. However, in the Book of Acts, God used people like Peter and Paul to extend the offer of salvation to *anyone* who wanted it. Afterward, restart the party—for all of your group members.

Step 5

Say: **Being a witness for Christ doesn't always come naturally. Sometimes we need to be reminded of our responsibility.** Bring in some art supplies—markers, construction paper, glue, pieces of felt cloth, buttons, etc. Instruct kids to create something that will remind them that they are witnesses for Christ. Their creation should be small enough that they can carry it around with them—or even attach to a belt loop or shoelace. Give kids a few minutes to work. Then have each person display and explain his or her creation.

MEDIA

Step 1

Show scenes (which you've screened beforehand) from *The Robe* or *Ben-Hur,* each of which is set in New Testament times. While these movies are Hollywood versions of reality, they do make some effort to depict the look of Palestine in the first century A.D. The scenes you choose should simply help kids envision those days—climate, terrain, houses, how people dressed and traveled, etc.—rather than raising specific issues. Ask: **How might the life of a Christian teenager have been harder then than it is now? How might it have been easier? What ways of spreading the Good News about Jesus do we have today that they didn't have then? How do you think the church managed to grow in an environment like that?**

Step 2

At the end of Step 2, play a song that the post-Pentecost disciples might identify with—"Nothing's Gonna Stop Us Now" by Starship. Ask: **How does this song make you feel? Other than the romantic overtones, how could it apply to the disciples?** At the end of Step 4, play a song Paul might identify with—"(I've Had) the Time of My Life" by Bill Medley and Jennifer Warnes. Ask: **Other than the romantic overtones, how is this like the message of II Timothy 4:6-8?** In Step 5, play "Nothing's Gonna Stop Us Now" again. Ask: **What parts of this song could represent your response to the Book of Acts? How could it be a "theme song" for our group?**

SHORT MEETING TIME

Step 1

Skip Step 1. Before the session, go to a toy store, variety store, or gift shop and find some compressed-sponge shapes—the kind that slowly grow much larger than their original tiny size when placed in water. Buy enough so that each person will have one. Give kids these compressed shapes as they enter. Each person should put his or hers in a water-filled gallon jar or fish tank that you've placed at the front of the room. Let kids keep track of the shapes' growth—a reminder of the early church's growth—as you work your way through the session. In Step 2, skip Repro Resource 2. Simply remind kids that there had been only two months between Palm Sunday and Pentecost. Summarize what happened at Pentecost.

Step 3

Skip Acts 10:9-23 and Acts 15:5-12. Use only Acts 11:1-18. In Step 4, save time by dividing the group seven ways (doubling up if necessary); assign each person or team to look for only one of the seven items on Repro Resource 3. After a few minutes, have kids share their findings.

URBAN

Step 2

You'll need four large maps of your city or urban area. Divide (using a marker) each map into four sections. Highlight a different section on each map. After you talk about Jesus' sending His disciples into all parts of the world, discuss how your group can begin to spread Christ's message throughout the city. Have kids form four teams. Give a map to each team. Instruct the members of each team to discuss how your group could spread the Gospel to the area highlighted on their map. They should identify any "problem spots" in the area (places with heavy gang activity), any "needy spots" (places with homelss shelters), etc. Then they should come up with a strategy for spreading the Gospel to that area, incorporating the "problem spots" and "needy spots" in their strategy.

Step 3

Play some video clips (which you've screened beforehand) that illustrate the racism and segregation that have been prevalent throughout our society's history. (Perhaps you might show scenes from *Roots, Glory,* and/or *Mississippi Burning.*) After you've shown the clips, point out that similar segregation took place in New Testament times. Just as people tried to keep African-Americans out of the "club"—whether the club was a restaurant, a hotel, a rest room, a section of a bus, etc.—first-century Jews tried to keep Gentiles out of the "club" of receiving God's blessings.

Combined Jr. High/High School

Step 1
At the beginning of the session, designate your high schoolers to be Gentiles and your junior highers to be Jews. But don't explain why you're giving these designations. Have your group members start playing the "initial game" according to the instructions in the session. However, after the two "initializers" finish claiming members for their respective teams, count how many of their "converts" are "Gentiles" (high schoolers). Subtract the number of Gentiles from each team's final membership and declare a winner. Afterward, point out that this was something like the mentality of the early church. Christianity was spreading like wildfire, but not for the Gentiles. At first, they were treated as if they didn't deserve to receive Christianity.

Step 5
Set up a competition in which your junior highers can challenge your high schoolers in a Bible-memorization contest. (If one age group is much larger than the other, have the larger group divide into two or more teams to compete.) Have each team line up single file. Hand a Bible to the first person in each line. Instruct that person to look up and memorize Acts 1:8. Once the person has it memorized, he or she should recite it several times to the second person in line, until the second person has it memorized. Teams should continue this process until all of its members have the verse memorized. The first team to have all of its members recite the verse to you is the winner. [NOTE: If you find that memorizing the entire verse at one time is difficult for your kids, allow them to memorize it phrase by phrase.] Afterward, discuss what it means to be Christ's "witnesses."

Sixth Grade

Step 2
Ask: **What are some things that "spread"?** (The flu, poison ivy, unkept secrets, rumors about other people, etc.) **Do you think bad things spread easier than good things? Explain.** Point out that a lot of people think it's tough to "spread the Gospel" (tell others about Jesus). However, there's a story in Acts in which the Gospel was spread like crazy. Have kids take turns reading Acts 2. Focus especially on verse 41 to see how many people were added to the number of believers during Pentecost. Point out that being witnesses for Christ in those days was very hard. People who tried to share the Gospel were stoned, imprisoned, beaten—all for "spreading" a good thing. Ask: **What are some problems people face today in trying to spread the Gospel?** Get a couple of responses. Encourage your kids to spread the Good News by treating people how Jesus would treat them and by being open to sharing that God loves them.

Step 4
It might be tough to hold some sixth graders' attention with Repro Resource 3. So rather than having kids fill out the sheet, share with them some of the more popular or more exciting stories about Paul and his preaching experiences. After each one, ask your kids what things in the story—both good and bad for Paul—stick out in their mind. Then have kids name some possible consequences, both good and bad, that might result from trying to be a Christian witness like Paul.

Planning Checklist

Date Used:

Approx. Time

Step 1: The Initial Activity _____
o Small Group
o Media
o Short Meeting Time
o Combined Jr. High/High School

Step 2: Spreading Like a Wildfire _____
o Extra Action
o Large Group
o Heard It All Before
o Little Bible Background
o Fellowship & Worship
o Mostly Girls
o Media
o Urban
o Sixth Grade

Step 3: Who's in the Club? _____
o Extra Action
o Large Group
o Little Bible Background
o Mostly Girls
o Mostly Guys
o Extra Fun
o Short Meeting Time
o Urban

Step 4: Paul: Up Close and Personal _____
o Small Group
o Heard It All Before
o Sixth Grade

Step 5: Can I Get a Witness? _____
o Fellowship & Worship
o Mostly Guys
o Extra Fun
o Combined Jr. High/High School

SESSION 3

What Every Christian Should Know—Part I (Romans—Philemon)

YOUR GOALS FOR THIS SESSION:

Choose one or more

- ☐ To help kids become familiar with the epistles of Paul.
- ☐ To help kids understand the basic foundations of Christian theology.
- ☐ To encourage kids to live creatively for Christ.
- ☐ Other ____________________

Your Bible Base:

Selected passages from Romans, I Corinthians, II Corinthians, Galatians, Ephesians, Philippians, Colossians, I Thessalonians, II Thessalonians, I Timothy, II Timothy, Titus, and Philemon

STEP 1

'Cause You've Got Personality

(Needed: Copies of Repro Resource 4, pencils, chalkboard and chalk or newsprint and marker)

OPTIONS

EXTRA ACTION
SMALL GROUP
LARGE GROUP
MOSTLY GUYS
MEDIA
SHORT MEETING TIME
SIXTH GRADE

Say: **There are two kinds of people in the world. What are they?** Give your kids a minute or two to come up with some creative divisions. For instance, one of them might suggest "those who think *The Simpsons* is funny and those who don't." Another might suggest "those who think a potato chip is a vegetable and those who don't."

After several group members have responded, say: **The two groups I was thinking of are those who divide everyone into two kinds of people and those who don't.** After you get a few groans, explain: **Actually, today we'll be looking at *eleven* kinds of people—and we'll try to figure out where each of us fits in.**

Hand out copies of "Personality Models" (Repro Resource 4) and pencils. As a group, read through the eleven different "personality models," pausing after each one to let group members fill in the names of people they know who fit that description.

After you've gone through the Repro Resource as a group, have group members write on the back of the sheet the model that most closely applies to them. Then, if your group members know each other fairly well, have them try to guess each other's personality model. If your group members don't know each other very well, have each person briefly explain which model he or she chose and why. If you have a lot of people in your group, you might want to have kids form small groups for this activity.

After everyone's personality model has been revealed (including your own), explain: **Each of these personality models corresponds to one of the books in the Bible written by Paul. Paul's books are actually letters that he wrote to various churches and people. Many of us probably had difficulty pinning ourselves down to one personality type, because we act differently in different situations. The same was true of Paul. As he wrote to different churches and people, he dealt with different situations. Therefore, each letter takes on its own personality.**

Have each group member try to figure out which of Paul's epistles (letters) matches his or her personality. It's not hard to interpret the code.

C1=I Corinthians
C2=II Corinthians
CO=Colossians
E=Ephesians
G=Galatians
PHL=Philippians
PHM=Philemon
R=Romans
TH=I & II Thessalonians
TM=I & II Timothy
TT=Titus

Write this key on the board so group members can refer to it later in the session.

STEP 2

Take a Letter

(Needed: Bibles, copies of Repro Resource 5, pencils)

Hand out copies of "Paul's Letters: Fact Sheet" (Repro Resource 5). Instruct each group member to find the epistle that most closely matches his or her personality model, read the information on the sheet about it, and then look up the key passages that are listed. It's OK if more than one group member chooses the same epistle; but if you have four or five kids working on the same book, you may want to ask some of them to choose another epistle—perhaps one that matches a "secondary" personality model. If you have a small group, you might want to have group members choose more than one epistle to work on. If possible, make sure each epistle is being covered by at least one of your group members.

Give the kids a few minutes to work. When everyone is finished, ask for a report on each epistle, beginning from Romans. Ask group members who covered each book to rephrase key passages in their own words and to describe how those passages deal with the situation facing the readers. Use the following information to supplement your discussion of the epistles.

Romans—The key passages present Paul's passion for the Gospel (1:16), *everyone's* need for forgiveness (3:23, 24), and a call for life commitment (12:1). The reference to a "living sacrifice" is in contrast to the dead animal sacrifices of Jewish tradition.

OPTIONS

I Corinthians—Church divisions make no sense, since we can only boast of what God is doing in us (1:31). Purity is crucial, even in the midst of evil (6:19, 20). Note that the Corinthians would contrast the Spirit's "temple" with local temples to pagan goddesses. Above all, Christian behavior must be characterized by love (13:1-3).

II Corinthians—At the beginning of the book, Paul makes an effort to comfort his readers (1:3, 4). Later, he defends his ministry, while still maintaining a humble attitude (4:1-7). He shows how the power of Christ is demonstrated through weakness (12:9).

Galatians—The cross was crucial to the Gospel (2:20). If one can be saved by the law, Christ's crucifixion was meaningless (3:1-3). The cross breaks down the walls between people-groups (3:28) and leads us into a Spirit-controlled life (5:22, 23).

Ephesians—The beginning of chapter 2 is about as concise a presentation of the Gospel as you'll find, culminating in the right understanding of human works (2:8, 9). This letter is full of pep talks (3:20, 21) and "warm fuzzies" (5:19, 20).

Philippians—Philippians 1:6 should be taped on every young person's bedroom mirror. God isn't finished with us yet. In tough times, we can learn from Christ's example (2:5-11) and trust in God's peace (4:6, 7).

Colossians—Paul focuses on Christ, amid the crazy teachings of others (1:18-20), and warns against "hollow" philosophy (2:8). Christians should live on a higher plane (3:1) and please God in all they do (3:17).

I & II Thessalonians—Paul describes Christ's return (I Thessalonians 4:16-18), but also gives practical guidelines for living (I Thessalonians 5:16-18; II Thessalonians 3:10). Christians should be future-minded but present-active.

I & II Timothy—Paul reaffirms the basic Gospel message (I Timothy 1:15), which the church must hang on to. He urges Timothy not to let his youth keep him from serving (4:12), but to work hard at pleasing God (II Timothy 2:15) and to remember his heritage (3:14-17).

Titus—Titus 2:11-14 combines visionary, practical, and doctrinal elements. All three are necessary for a growing church. Paul points out that anyone—even the morally bankrupt Cretans—can be transformed by Christ (3:3-8).

Philemon—With warmth and humor, Paul shows how much he values a slave and then zeroes in on the terms of Onesimus's return (10-16).

After group members have reported, say: **Sometimes we think of the Bible as just a rule book in which God tells us how to live. That's not the whole story. It was written at different times to people in different situations. The original readers found help in it for some very tough problems and questions.**

Does that mean it has nothing to say to us today? Absolutely not! Our problems are not so different from those of first-century Christians. We can find greater meaning in Scripture when we understand its original context. For

instance, Philippians 4:6 tells us not to be anxious about anything, but to pray about it. We might say, "Yeah, yeah. Religious stuff. Been there, done that." But when we realize that Paul wrote this while under house arrest in Rome, not knowing when he might be executed or freed, it gives a whole new power to the verse.

In His wisdom, God allows us to learn from those who have gone before—and He teaches us from what He taught them.

STEP 3

All Roads Lead to Rome

(Needed: Two copies of Repro Resource 6)

Ask: **What's the difference between the Gospels and the Epistles in what they tell us about Jesus?** (Generally, the Gospels tell us what Jesus *said* and *did*. The Epistles tell us who He *was* and what He *meant*. The Gospels give us the facts of history. The Epistles show how those facts matter to us.)

Say: **Let's take a closer look at one of Paul's epistles—Romans. Rome was the bustling center of a great empire. Paul knew that, and he probably had an extra motivation when he wrote to the church in Rome, knowing that many people would come in contact with this influential church. He wanted to present the clearest explanation possible of why people need to trust Christ. And he composed a masterpiece. We can follow his logic by picking verses here and there throughout Romans. Some people call this the "Romans Road."**

Ask for two volunteers to perform a skit. Give each of them a copy of "The Romans Road" (Repro Resource 6). You'll also need to assign group members to read Scripture passages throughout the skit. The script calls for eight different readers; but if your group is small, you could double up on lines and have four people do it. Distribute copies of Repro Resource 6 to all of your readers.

During the skit, "A" will cue each reader by pushing a button on his or her imaginary computer. Readers should be lined up so that they know who's next.

After the skit has been performed, say: **The Book of Romans says**

OPTIONS

a lot about our relationship with God. Maybe you're at a point where you need to stop relying on your own efforts and start trusting in Christ. This would be a great time to invite Christ into your life.

Or maybe you just need the reassurance that Jesus does forgive you for whatever sins you've committed. There is "no condemnation" for Christians, so get things straightened out with Him.

Or maybe you need a kick in the pants. You're a Christian, but you're living like you don't know God. Why play dead when you can have such a great life?

STEP 4

Dear Me

(Needed: Paper, pencils)

OPTIONS

Make sure all of your group members have pencils and paper. (They may use the back of one of their Repro Resources if necessary.) Ask: **If Paul were to write a letter to you, what might it say? Or if God were to send you a message, what might it be?**

Group members should start with their "situation." Are they like the Corinthians, facing difficult questions of how to live for Christ in a wicked world? Are they like the Galatians, mulling over basic questions about what Christ has done for us? Are they like the Philippians, facing some tough times? Or are they like the Ephesians, in pretty good shape? Instruct group members to write a few brief comments describing their situation.

Then ask them to write down what message God might send them. Perhaps it's a verse that was read in this session or some other Scripture passage they know. Perhaps it's some other sort of assurance or challenge. Give group members a few minutes to think about this. Afterward, ask for volunteers to share what they wrote. (However, *do not force* anyone to share.)

Then close the session in prayer, asking God to continue communicating with your group members, instructing, guiding, and comforting them.

PeRSOnAlity MoDeLs

C1 Model
Practical; applies workable solutions to difficult problems.
Someone I know who is like this: ______________________________

C2 Model
Peacemaker; promotes unity among others; comforts; smoothes over differences.
Someone I know who is like this: ______________________________

CO Model
Discerner; sees the errors in wrong ideas and convinces people to move in good directions.
Someone I know who is like this: ______________________________

E Model
Group builder; gets people to work together; encourages people to use their gifts.
Someone I know who is like this: ______________________________

G Model
Passionate for the truth; hates to see people deceived; says what he or she thinks.
Someone I know who is like this: ______________________________

PHL Model
Joyful; looks at the bright side even in bad situations.
Someone I know who is like this: ______________________________

PHM Model
Advocate; speaks out on behalf of others, especially those less fortunate.
Someone I know who is like this: ______________________________

R Model
Very logical; thinks through important issues.
Someone I know who is like this: ______________________________

TH Model
Future-minded; always thinking about things to come—and rather hopeful about them.
Someone I know who is like this: ______________________________

TM Model
Young, but has a lot of potential; knows he or she has a lot to learn, but eagerly seeks out new experiences.
Someone I know who is like this: ______________________________

TT Model
Leader; disciplined and responsible; serves as an example to others.
Someone I know who is like this: ______________________________

Paul's Letters: FACT SHEET

ROMANS

Readers: The people of the church at Rome. Rome was the capital of the Roman Empire. Paul had never been there, but knew many Christians who had moved there.
Situation: The church was made up of both Jews and Gentiles. There were probably some questions about how Christianity should interact with Jewish traditions.
Key Passages: Romans 1:16; 3:23, 24; 12:1

I CORINTHIANS

Readers: The people of the church at Corinth. Corinth was a business center of the Roman Empire, and was known for its loose morals and idol worship. Paul had helped to start the church there and stayed for a year and a half (Acts 18:1-11).
Situation: The church was facing the problem of divison among its members. The church members were also being tempted by the immorality of the city around them.
Key Passages: I Corinthians 1:31; 6:19, 20; 13:1-3

II CORINTHIANS

Readers: Same as I Corinthians.
Situation: False teachers had infiltrated the church and were questioning Paul's integrity and authority. Paul wanted to comfort the Corinthians and reassure them that he was honorable and that his message of life-changing salvation was true.
Key Passages: II Corinthians 1:3, 4; 4:1-7; 12:9

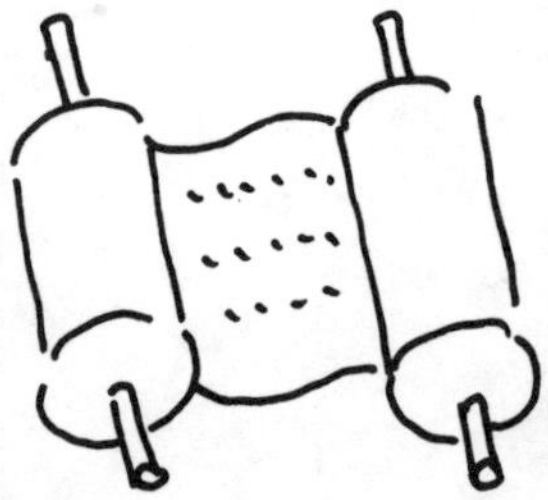

GALATIANS

Readers: The people of the churches throughout the region of Galatia. We're not entirely sure where this was, though it may have been the area Paul visited on his first missionary journey (Acts 13–14). In any case, these were inland villages, not major cities on the coast.
Situation: Paul had taught a simple gospel of salvation by faith alone. But other teachers came after him, claiming that Gentiles had to become Jews in order to be acceptable.
Key Passages: Galatians 2:20; 3:1-3, 28; 5:22, 23

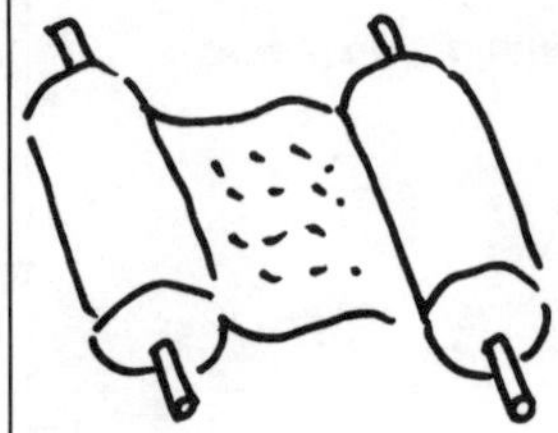

EPHESIANS

Readers: The people of the church at Ephesus. Ephesus was a major city on the Aegean coast. It was a center for worship of the pagan goddess Artemis (Diana). Paul had made it a second home in his travels, staying there three years.
Situation: The church was in pretty good shape, needing only a "brush up" on the basics of Christian faith and life.
Key Passages: Ephesians 2:8, 9; 3:20, 21; 5:19, 20

PHILIPPIANS

Readers: The people of the church at Philippi. Philippi was a Roman colony, and most of its church members were Gentiles.
Situation: Paul was imprisoned, and the Philippians had sent him a gift. Paul writes back to thank and reassure them.
Key Passages: Philippians 1:6; 2:5-11; 4:6, 7

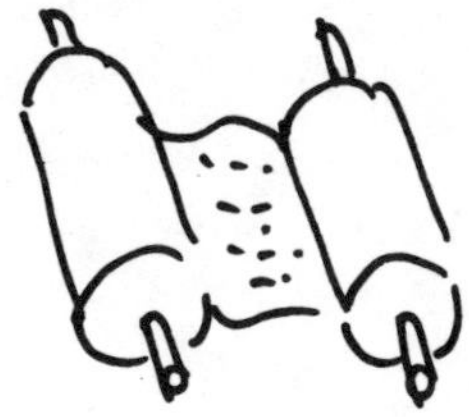

COLOSSIANS

Readers: The people of the church at Colosse. Colosse was a town in what is now Turkey. Epaphras, an associate of Paul, had started the church there.
Situation: There was a sort of "New Age movement" in the area. Teachers were promising the fullness of God through praying to angels and following strict rituals. Paul had to defuse this explosive teaching.
Key Passages: Colossians 1:18-20; 2:8; 3:1, 17

I & II THESSALONIANS

Readers: The people of the church at Thessalonica. Thessalonica was a major city in northern Greece. Paul had visited there on his second journey (Acts 17:1-9).
Situation: The Thessalonians had a question about believers who died: What happens to them? In the first letter, Paul tells them of Christ's return. But they apparently misunderstood—quitting their jobs and sitting on rooftops, etc.—so Paul urges patience in the second letter.
Key Passages: I Thessalonians 4:16-18; 5:16-18; II Thessalonians 3:10

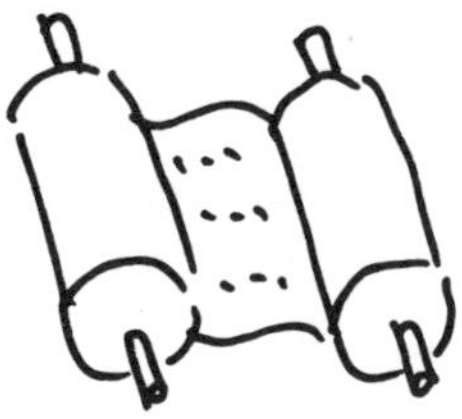

I & II TIMOTHY

Reader: Timothy, who had traveled as a missionary with Paul. At the time of these letters, Timothy was a young pastor in Ephesus.
Situation: Paul was concerned about the doctrine of the church, the behavior of Christians, and the development of strong church leaders. He also missed having Timothy around.
Key Passages: I Timothy 1:15; 4:12; II Timothy 2:15; 3:14-17

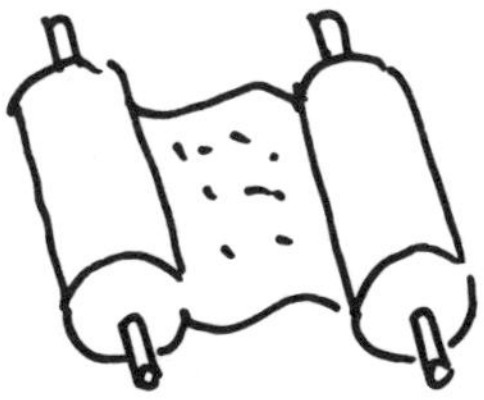

TITUS

Reader: Titus, who was a Gentile converted through Paul's ministry. Paul developed him as a church leader, and installed him as a pastor in Crete.
Situation: Pastoring the church in Crete was a tough assignment for Titus. Paul writes to encourage and instruct him.
Key Passages: Titus 2:11-14; 3:3-8

PHILEMON

Reader: Philemon, who was a member of the church at Colosse.
Situation: Philemon's slave, Onesimus, escaped and ran off to Rome, where Paul led him to Christ. Paul sends Onesimus back with this letter, asking Philemon to forgive him fully.
Key Passages: Philemon 10-16

THE ROMANS ROAD

A: My friend, with the help of this machine, I will now take you down the Romans Road.
B: What's that?
A: The simple truth of the Gospel, condensed into a handful of verses, all from the Book of Romans. I'll just fire up my CD-ROME here, and we'll listen to the computer recite these verses. Here we go. *(Pushes button.)*
READER 1: *READS ROMANS 1:20, 21.*
B: That's great!
A: Sounded kind of depressing to me.
B: No, the machine. That's amazing.
A: But did you understand those verses?
B: Something about creation.
A: God has built the knowledge of Himself into His creation, so that any dolt can look around and know that there's a God. Even you.
B: Thanks. Hey, I believe in God. I just don't believe in the existence of atheists.
A: Some people can see there's a God, but they deny it.
B: Not me. I was raised in a good home. I've believed in God since I was two. I'm glad I'm not like those people the computer was talking about.
A: Funny you should say that. *(Presses button.)*
READER 2: *READS ROMANS 2:1.*
B: Well, nobody's perfect.
A: Exactamundo! *(Pushes button.)*
READER 3: *READS ROMANS 3:23.*
B: OK, OK. But I figure if I try to live a good life, God will love me anyway. Isn't that how it works?
A: Not really. *(Pushes button.)*
READER 4: *READS ROMANS 5:8.*
A: You see, God loves sinners. You have to come to Him as a sinner, not trying to earn your own way. *After* we trust Him, He helps us to live better. But we are saved by God's grace, not by our good behavior.
B: So then it doesn't matter how we live? I can do whatever I want and still be forgiven?
A: Yes and no. *(Pushes button.)*
READER 5: *READS ROMANS 6:1, 2.*
A: God forgives us, but He also changes us. He sets us free from the control of sin.
B: OK, so I trust Christ. And for a while I live a good life, but then I screw up. What then?
A: Gotcha covered. *(Pushes button.)*
READER 6: *READS ROMANS 8:1.*
B: "No condemnation." I like that.
A: Yes, those in Christ are accepted and acceptable. *(Pushes button.)*
READER 7: *READS ROMANS 8:38, 39.*
B: So how do I tap into the love of God? Is there some sort of ritual I need to follow?
A: Nope. It's pretty simple. *(Pushes button.)*
READER 8: *READS ROMANS 10:9.*
B: I'll do it. That's a great machine you've got there. What do you call it?
A: Oh, I just call it a "Catalytic Converter."

EXTRA ACTION

Step 1
Play "Air Compressor"—because you'll be compressing a lot of Scripture into a little time. Have kids form two teams. Give each team a large cardboard carton (the bigger the better) and a supply of balloons (the more the merrier) inflated to roughly equal size. See which team can stuff more balloons in its carton without popping any. Give the winning team a prize.

Step 3
Instead of the computer skit, go with the "Romans Road" idea. Before the session, write each of the eight passages on a sheet of poster board, minus references. On the other side of each sheet, write a portion of the following Burma Shave-style poem. The first portion should be on the back of the Romans 1:20, 21 sheet; the second portion should be on the back of the Romans 2:1 sheet; etc., so that both the poem portions and the passages are in the same order. Here's the poem: "Just Be Alert / On the Romans Road / And You Won't Squash / Some Helpless Toad / Or Miss a Chance / To Be Like Paul / And Share the Word / With One and All." Pass out the sheets. Give the group one minute to figure out the correct order of the sheets, using the poem, and place them on the floor to form a "road." Then turn the sheets over and discuss the concept of the Romans Road. Walk down the "road" together, asking volunteers to paraphrase the passages aloud.

SMALL GROUP

Step 1
With a small group, it's likely that your group members know each other fairly well. So rather than having each person determine his or her own personality model, allow the other group members to decide for him or her. One at a time, bring each group member to the front of the room. While he or she stands "on display," have the rest of the kids huddle together and decide which personality model fits him or her. After the group reaches a consensus, allow the person to agree or disagree with the group's choice. (However, disagreeing will do no good, since the group's decision stands.) Because all of the personality models are worded positively, an added benefit of this activity is that kids will feel encouraged to be thought of by the group in such a positive way.

Step 2
In addition to having kids work on the book that corresponds with the personality model chosen by the rest of the group (see the option above), you'll also need to assign one or two other books to each person. Make sure all of the books on Repro Resource 5 are covered. As group members report on their assigned book(s), they should do so in first-person style. For instance, the person covering Colossians might say, "Hi. I'm from the church at Colosse. We've got some problems in our church right now. Some teachers in the area are saying that we can achieve the "fullness of God" by praying to angels and by following a bunch of strict rituals. You can imagine that Paul wasn't very happy when he heard about this. As a matter of fact, we just got a letter from Paul yesterday. Listen to some of things he says." The person would then read the key passages from the book.

LARGE GROUP

Step 1
With a large group, you may not have time for everyone to explain his or her personality type to the rest of the group. Instead, divide your room into eleven sections. Designate each section as one of the personality models listed on Repro Resource 4. Once group members have determined which personality model best describes them, they should go to the appropriate area. (If a section has only one person in it, have that person merge with another group.) Instruct each group member to share with the others in his or her section why he or she fits that personality model. Then ask: **Considering your personality type, what's the best way for someone to communicate something to you? What if what the person has to say is something you don't want to hear?** Use this discussion to introduce the topic of how Paul used different methods for communicating to different churches.

Step 2
Have kids form small groups. Assign one or more (depending on how many small groups you have) of the books (or groups of books) on Repro Resource 5 to each group. Instruct each small group to come up with a memorable way to present its book (and the relevant information about the book) to the rest of the group. For instance, for Philemon, group members might get down on their knees during their presentation to indicate that Philemon is the *shortest* of Paul's letters; one of the group members might have his or her hands tied to indicate that Philemon was an escaped slave. Other groups may use cheers, poems, skits, puns, etc. to present their books. After all of the books have been presented, have the group vote on which presentation was most memorable. Award prizes to the winning group.

Step 2

Kids may think it's OK to know the names of Bible books and maybe their order—but that it's unnecessary to know what's in each book. Challenge this idea by writing on the board the following string of names and asking the group to memorize it: "Benzocaine Tetracycline Lidocaine Acetaminophin L-dopa Ampicillin Ceclor Dextromethorphan Prozac Bismuth." Don't offer a prize for memorization. If kids balk, ask why. They'll probably object because there's little to be gained by remembering the words. If kids try to memorize the words, congratulate them but ask what good it did them. Explain that the list was made up of medicines. Just as it's good to know what's on the label of a medicine bottle, it's good to know the labels for Bible books and their order. But labels are just the beginning. To know where to go when we need help, we need to know what's behind the labels.

Step 3

Christian kids may think they don't need to hear these "salvation verses" again. If most of your group falls into this category, approach the "Romans Road" as a compact way to summarize the Good News for a friend. After using the skit, have kids tab their Bibles with numbered Post-It™ notes to help them find the verses quickly. Or you might have them design bookmarks that list the references.

Step 2

Names like "Corinthians," "Philippians," and "Thessalonians" may seem strange and confusing to someone who is new to the Bible. Conduct a brief exercise to help kids understand what these names are. Ask: **If Paul had written to the people of the church of Florida, what might his letter have been called?** (Floridians?) **If he'd written to the people of the church of Toronto, what might his letter have been called?** (Torontians?) Continue with places like Walla Walla (Washington), Kalamazoo (Michigan), Anaheim (California), etc. Afterward, give kids a few minutes to come up with an acrostic phrase (or phrases) to help them remember the order of the Pauline epistles. After a few minutes, have each person share his or her phrase(s). Award a prize for "Most Original Acrostic."

Step 3

In a skit format, the material on Repro Resource 6 may get lost on kids who aren't familiar with the Bible. It would be a shame if the "Romans Road" presentation was marred by a bad line reading or because someone was concentrating on his or her own lines. So rather than using the skit, present the "Romans Road" material in a clear, concise, straightforward manner. Have someone read the first verse; then briefly discuss what it means as a group. (Use the material on Repro Resource 6 as necessary to guide your discussion.) If possible, you might even create a "Romans Road" handout for your kids to take home. On it, write the eight passages from Repro Resource 6, as well as a brief explanation of each passage. Ask: **Do you think this "Romans Road" material would be useful if and when you talk to others about Christ? Why or why not?**

Step 2

Before the session, cut out *only* the personality descriptions (for example, "Practical; applies workable solutions to difficult problems") from Repro Resource 4. Distribute these among your group members. Also cut apart the descriptions of Paul's letters (one book per slip) from Repro Resource 5. Distribute these as well. Have kids mingle and see whether they can match the epistles and personalities. When a match is made, the two group members should read together the key passages from the book.

Step 4

As you wrap up the session, lead your group members in singing a couple of hymns and/or choruses that are based on passages or themes from Paul's letters. Among the hymns and choruses you might consider using are "I've Got the Joy, Joy, Joy, Joy Down in My Heart," "Blest Be the Tie That Binds," and "The Church's One Foundation."

MOSTLY GIRLS

Step 2
Ask your girls to share about a time when they received help for a problem from someone who had been through a similar situation. If they're reluctant to share with the whole group, have them write down their examples. Then collect the examples and read them aloud without identifying who wrote them. Ask: **When you're struggling with a situation or problem, why do you think it helps to talk to someone who's been through a similar situation? Do you think that has anything to do with why Jesus came to earth as a human being? Explain.**

Step 3
At the beginning of Step 3, to make the difference between the Gospels and Epistles a little more clear, have your girls make two columns on a sheet of paper. At the top of one column, have them write "Who I Am"; at the top of the other column, have them write "What I Do." Challenge them to fill in as many lines under each column as they can. Many of your girls may never have thought of the difference between who we are and what we do; they may need some help getting started. Emphasize that God loves us for who we are, regardless of what we do.

MOSTLY GUYS

Step 1
Your guys may be reluctant to divulge their own personality model to the group. Instead, have them play "Celebrity Personality-Model Matchup." As a group, go through Repro Resource 4 and match up the personality models with celebrities (either real or fictional) who fit those descriptions. For instance, the "R Model" would certainly apply to Mr. Spock (of *Star Trek* fame); the "TM Model" might apply to Luke Skywalker (from the *Star Wars* trilogy). Write the matches on the board as group members call them out. Later, as you assign the books, use the celebrity tie-ins (**Jeff, you take Mr. Spock's book. Tony, you take Luke Skywalker's . . .**).

Step 2
To help your guys become familiar with the order of Pauline letters, conduct a timed contest. You'll need thirteen shoeboxes (each with the title of one of Paul's letters written on its side), a Bible, and a stopwatch. Put the Bible at one end of the room and the shoeboxes at the other end. When you say, **Go** (and start timing), the first contestant will run to the Bible, look up the order of the books, and then run to the boxes to stack them in order. If he gets confused, he must run back to the Bible, look at the order of the books again, and then run back to the boxes to make the necessary changes. As soon as he gets the boxes stacked in the correct order, stop the stopwatch. Write each contestant's time on the board. Award a prize to the person who correctly stacks the boxes in the shortest amount of time. [NOTE: As each contestant competes, make sure the rest of the guys don't have access to Bibles and that they can't see the order of the boxes being stacked. Otherwise, the final contestant would have an unfair advantage because he had time to memorize the books.]

EXTRA FUN

Step 2
Have a contest to see who can come up with the most words using the letters in the title of one of Paul's books. But to make things a little more difficult, add a catch to the game: The only words that may be used are ones that can be found in the book itself. For instance, if you use "Corinthians," kids may use only words that are found in I and II Corinthians ("this" [I Corinthians 4:14]; "thorn" [II Corinthians 12:7]; etc.). Play several rounds, as time allows, using different books.

Step 4
To close the session, have kids form teams for a quiz to see how much they remember about the material from this session. Make sure there are an equal number of players on each team. Have the first person from each team come to the front of the room for the first question. After you ask the question, contestants will "buzz in" by calling out their name. The first person to buzz in gets a chance to answer the question. If the person answers correctly, his or her team gets a point. If not, the other contestants will have a chance to buzz in. The questions may cover anything from the Pauline epistles. For example, you might describe a church's condition and ask which church you're describing. Or you might read a key verse and ask what book it's from. You might ask how "Galatians" is spelled. Or you might ask who the author of Romans is—just to see if you can catch someone off guard. Award prizes to the team that answers the most questions correctly.

MEDIA

Step 1
During the week before the session, videotape the first five minutes or so of a TV newscast. To start the meeting, show the tape. Then ask: **If you had to write a letter to each person mentioned in this newscast so far, what kinds of letters would you write?** You may want to list the people mentioned and divide them into categories (disaster victims, criminals, politicians, etc.) to aid kids' memories. Use this as an illustration of how Paul's letters had to differ according to the situations in which his readers found themselves.

Step 2
Have kids record a "condensed version" of these letters by quickly reading the verses and recording them on audiotape. Play the tape back in Step 4 as a review. In Step 3, pre-record the Romans verses and use the tape in the skit instead of using readers.

SHORT MEETING TIME

Step 1
Replace Step 1 with a shorter opener. Before the session, cut Repro Resource 5 into slips—one epistle per slip. Get enough letter-sized envelopes so that each group member will have one. Using a utility knife or razor blade, cut a slit in the bottom edge of each envelope. The slit should be hard to detect, just long enough for one of the slips to pass through end first. Put a slip in each envelope, making sure it doesn't fall through the slit. Seal each envelope. To start the meeting, give one envelope to each person. (Make more copies and cut them up if you have more than eleven group members; if you have fewer than eleven, hold the leftover slips yourself.) Explain: **There's a message in your envelope. You have one minute to get it out—without cutting or tearing the envelope. The first person to do this wins.** See whether kids find the slit and discover that they can pull the slip out with a finger. After the contest, ask: **When have you been most eager to get a real letter out of an envelope? Why?** Explain that you'll be looking at some special letters in this session. Then move into Step 2 by having each person look at the letter described on his or her slip. (Assign any leftover slips as well.)

Step 3
If you need to save a lot of time, skip Step 3. If not, condense the step as follows. Have kids pretend that they're stranded on a desert island. All they've heard of the Bible are the eight passages from Romans. Have volunteers read these. Then ask: **Would you know enough to receive Christ after reading these verses? If not, what more would you need to know? How could you use these verses to share your faith with a friend?**

URBAN

Step 3
To help illustrate the difference between the Gospels and the Epistles, have kids focus on a great cultural or religious figure they're familiar with. Among the cultural figures you might consider using are Geronimo, Harriet Tubman, Malcolm X, and Frederick Douglas. Among the religious figures you might consider using are Richard Allen, Billy Graham, and Matin Luther King, Jr. First, as a group, brainstorm a list of things the person said and/or did. Then discuss what the person's words and/or actions mean to us today. Point out that similarly, the Gospels tell us what Jesus said and did; the Epistles tell us what Jesus' words and deeds mean to us today.

Step 4
Some of your urban young people may be reluctant to make themselves "vulnerable" enough to write a letter to themselves. Instead, have them focus on what God might say to the teens of the city in general. What kind of message would He have for them? Would it be encouraging? Challenging? Full of hope? Full of stern warnings? Another option would be to set up a video camera in another room and have kids share their responses privately in front of the camera. Then after everyone has had a chance to share, play back the tape for your group. Your kids will probably love to see themselves on TV.

OPTIONS

SESSION THREE

Combined Jr. High/High School

Step 2
Have your junior highers and high schoolers compete in a "mnemonic" contest. Give each group eleven pieces of poster board and markers. See which group can create the best mnemonic (memory-aiding) picture for each book (or group of books) on Repro Resource 5. Each picture should convey as much information as possible. Kids may not use words in their pictures; the only numbers they may use are the references for key passages. For instance, a picture for Philippians might show a car at a gas pump ("*Fill-up*-ians"). The license plate of the car may read "1:6; 2:5-11; 4:6, 7" (the key passages). In the background, a man in jail is opening a present (representing Paul's receiving a gift in prison). A dotted line connects that scene to a scene in which a person is stuffing fruit into a pie (representing that the gift came from the people of "Fill-a-pie"). Give the groups several minutes to work. When they're finished, have each one present and explain its picture for each book. You'll judge which picture is best for each book and award a point to that group. The group with the most points at the end of the game is the winner.

Step 3
With your junior highers and high schoolers working in separate groups, have kids rewrite the "Romans Road" presentation on Repro Resource 6, specifically tailoring it for their peers. Have the members of each group look up the verses listed on the sheet and rewrite them to fit the specific situations of kids they know. (Junior highers will be writing for other junior highers; high schoolers will be writing for other high schoolers.) Encourage kids to use any terms, phrases, and non-offensive slang that is currently popular among their friends. After a few minutes, have each group share its creation.

Sixth Grade

Step 1
Rather than having your sixth graders try to identify their personality type and then match that type with one of Paul's letters, simply focus on why Paul wrote different kinds of letters to different churches. Ask: **How might a letter you write to your best friend be different from a letter you write to your grandmother? What kinds of things would you write about to your friend that you wouldn't write to your grandma? How might a letter you write to a pen pal overseas be different from a letter you write to a brother or sister at college?** Use this discussion to introduce Paul's letters to churches facing different circumstances.

Step 2
As a group, come up with a simple phrase (no more than three or four words) to summarize the information about each book (or group of books) on Repro Resource 5. For instance, you might use "Christianity and Jewish traditions" for Romans; "divisions and outside immorality" for I Corinthians; "false teachers vs. Paul" for II Corinthians; etc. Write the phrases on the board as you come up with them. Then give group members an opportunity to memorize the phrases. After a few minutes, erase or cover up the phrases. Then have each of your group members see how many phrases he or she can recall. You might want to award a prize to the person who can recite the most. Throughout the rest of the session, randomly "test" your kids to see how many phrases they still recall (e.g., **Kevin, what's the phrase for Philemon?**).

Planning Checklist

Date Used:

Approx. Time

Step 1: 'Cause You've Got Personality ______
o Extra Action
o Small Group
o Large Group
o Mostly Guys
o Media
o Short Meeting Time
o Sixth Grade

Step 2: Take a Letter ______
o Small Group
o Large Group
o Heard It All Before
o Little Bible Background
o Fellowship & Worship
o Mostly Girls
o Mostly Guys
o Extra Fun
o Media
o Combined Jr. High/High School
o Sixth Grade

Step 3: All Roads Lead to Rome ______
o Extra Action
o Heard It All Before
o Little Bible Background
o Mostly Girls
o Short Meeting Time
o Urban
o Combined Jr. High/High School

Step 4: Dear Me ______
o Fellowship & Worship
o Extra Fun
o Urban

SESSION 4

What Every Christian Should Know—Part II (Hebrews—Jude)

YOUR GOALS FOR THIS SESSION:

Choose one or more

- ☐ To help kids become familiar with the general epistles.
- ☐ To help kids understand what "Christian love" and "putting faith into action" involves.
- ☐ To encourage kids to put their faith into action and to show Christian love courageously.
- ☐ Other ______________________________

Your Bible Base:

Selected passages from Hebrews, James, I John, II John, III John, and Jude

STEP 1

Roleplay Mania

(Actors to perform to a couple of roleplays)

OPTIONS

Sometime before the meeting, recruit three actors to perform a couple of roleplays for your group. If possible, try to find some adults in your church who have some stage experience. If you can't find anyone outside the group, recruit three of the better actors in your group to perform. If possible, meet with the actors a couple of days before the meeting to explain the roleplays and give the actors a chance to prepare.

Begin your session by having the actors perform. The roleplays are as follows:

Situation 1—"A," "B," and "C" are in an airplane. "A" is trying to convince "B" to jump out of the plane without a paracute. "C" is trying to convince "B" not to. "A" and "C" offer several arguments—some funny, some serious—as to why "B" should or shouldn't jump out of the plane. "B" considers the pros and cons, and then makes a final decision.

After the actors finish this roleplay, ask your group members: **Who do you think was showing the most concern for "B," the person who was deciding whether or not to jump? How did "A" and "C" treat each other as they tried to convince "B" what to do? Do you think the best thing to do in this situation would be to let "B" do whatever he (or she) wants? Explain.** The conclusion kids should reach is that doing what's best for someone sometimes involves pointing out the error of his or her ways and/or opposing those who are giving the person bad advice. (This roleplay will introduce the topic of showing Christian love to others.)

Situation 2—"A" is in a college admissions interview. The only problem is that "A" is dead. (This is an easy role to play.) "B," a friend, is trying to convince "C," the dean of admissions, that "A" should be accepted to the college. [NOTE: The dead-body scenario can be very funny—unless there's been a death in your immediate community recently. In that case, you can change "A" to an "imaginary friend." It's not quite the same, but it will work.]

After the actors finish this roleplay, ask your group members: **What were the most convincing arguments the friend offered for allowing the dead person into college? Why would a silly thing like death keep such a prize student from being accepted into college?** The conclusion group members should reach is that a dead person could not contribute much to campus life. (This roleplay will introduce the topic of how a "dead" faith—one that is just a matter of words and not deeds—contributes very little to the work of God.)

Give your actors a round of applause and dismiss them (if they're not members of your group).

STEP 2

Faith: The Facts

(Needed: Bibles, copies of Repro Resource 7, copies of Repro Resource 8, pencils, chalkboard and chalk or newsprint and marker)

Hand out copies of "General Letters: Fact Sheet" (Repro Resource 7) and pencils. Announce that for now, you'll be focusing on just the first two books—Hebrews and James. Have kids form two teams. Assign one team the Book of Hebrews and the other team the Book of James. (If yours is a large group, have kids form several teams. Then assign half of the teams the Book of Hebrews and the other half the Book of James.)

Instruct the teams to read the information on their book, look up the key passages, and come up with a "life principle"—something that would be helpful to a kid trying to live a Christian life—for each passage.

Give the teams a few minutes to work. When everyone is finished, have members of each team read aloud their key passages and explain the life principle they came up with for each one. Write these principles on the board under two headings: "Hebrews" and "James." Use the following information to supplement your discussion of the principles the teams came up with.

Hebrews 1:1-3—God speaks to us in Jesus. Jesus is the "exact representation" of God. Therefore, through Jesus, we have direct access to God because He provides purification.

Hebrews 4:15, 16—Jesus knows what it's like to be tempted. He was tempted throughout His life—yet He never gave in to sin. Therefore, when we're tempted, we can talk to Him about it and receive help from the only person who ever successfully resisted temptation for His entire life. We can be confident that we'll receive *real* help if we ask Him for it.

Hebrews 12:1-3—The Christian life is like a race. We may get tired sometimes as we run—and sin can hinder our performance. So we need to get rid of the things that "entangle" us and slow us down. We

OPTIONS

need to persevere and "keep running."

James 1:17—Everything good and "perfect" in our lives comes from God. And we can count on Him to continue supplying good and perfect things because He never changes.

James 1:22—If we merely "hear" God's Word (read it, listen to sermons about it, etc.) without doing what it says or applying it to our everyday situations, it's not going to make much difference in our lives.

James 4:7—When we give our lives completely to God, we have a foolproof tactic for battling the devil. If we stand firm in our commitment to God and resist the devil's temptations, Satan will run away from us.

Explain that the Book of Hebrews is like a really good sermon that helps us make sense of the various aspects of the Christian life. The Book of James, on the other hand, is like a playbook that gives us specific instructions on how Christians should live—what we should and shouldn't do. Point out that both books share a common theme: faith. Hebrews has an entire chapter (11) devoted to faith, and James gives us an interesting angle on the topic.

Have everyone turn to Hebrews 11. Ask volunteers to read aloud verses 1, 2, 7, 17, 18, and 23.

Explain: **The author of Hebrews uses Old Testament examples of faith. We just read a few of them, but what do they have in common?** (Motivated by faith, these people *did something*. Encouraged by their trust in God, they attempted—and accomplished—bold deeds.)

Have everyone turn to James 2:14-18. Ask someone to read it aloud. Then say: **Back in the Book of Romans, Paul tells us that we can't do anything to earn our salvation, that it's a gift of God. Now this passage seems to be saying that we can't be saved unless we do good works. What's the deal?** (God's grace saves us, and we accept it in faith. We can't do anything to earn it. That faith then produces good deeds in us. James is working backward here. He's saying that if someone is not producing good deeds, it's an indication that faith is not at work in his or her life.)

To demonstrate this point, ask for a guy and a girl to perform a brief skit. Give each volunteer a copy of "The Visitor" (Repro Resource 8). After giving the actors a minute to read through the script, have them perform the skit.

Afterward, ask: **Does this mean that when we sin or when we neglect to do a good deed for someone, we're not saved anymore?** (James is saying that true faith reveals itself in good deeds. If those good deeds are not present, it indicates that something is wrong with what we're calling faith. God will forgive our sins if we ask Him to. But if there is no desire within us to do good deeds, we need to take a serious look at the nature of our faith.)

Ask: **What do you think Ann, the girl in the skit, should do**

now? (Commit herself to Christ. Whether this is her point of salvation or a recommitment of her life is open to debate. Either way, she needs to do it in order to develop a lively faith.)

Refer back to the second roleplay at the beginning of the session. Point out that a "dead" faith—one that is not accompanied by action—is of about as much use to God as a dead student would be to a college.

STEP 3

Love, Biblical Style

(Needed: Bibles, copies of Repro Resource 7)

Ask: **According to Jesus, what are the two greatest commandments?** If your group members don't know the answer, refer them to Matthew 22:34-40. Jesus said, "'Love the Lord your God with all your heart and with all your soul and with all your mind.' This is the first and greatest commandment. And the second is like it: 'Love your neighbor as yourself.'"

Ask: **When you think of love, what kinds of images come to mind?** Explain that love doesn't always involve "gooey" feelings and gentle words. Then point out that the last six epistles in the New Testament have a lot to say about love.

Refer group members again to Repro Resource 7. Then have them form four teams. Assign the first team I Peter; the second team II Peter; the third team I John; and the fourth team II John, III John, and Jude.

Instruct the teams to read the key passages for their book and answer this question: **What can we learn from these passages about Christian love?**

Give the teams a few minutes to work. When everyone is finished, have each team share its response. Use the following information to supplement the teams' responses.

I Peter—Our love for God results in holiness, because He is holy (1:15, 16). We praise God out of our love for Him (2:9). We demonstrate our love for others by sharing Christ with them and being prepared to answer their questions about Him (3:15, 16). We trust in the fact that God loves and cares for us (5:7).

II Peter—Our love is grounded in the truth of God, not in human imaginations (1:20, 21). Our love needs to be patient—even long-suffering—as God is (3:8, 9).

O P T I O N S

I John—Our love for the Lord keeps us in contact with Him, confessing our sins when we mess up (1:5-9). True love is sacrificial, especially when it comes to helping people in need (3:16, 17). Our love comes from God; we are able to love only because He loved us first (4:10, 19).

II & III John—Love leads us to obey God (II John 6). Love for God helps us discern between good and evil—and follow good (III John 11).

Have someone read III John 9 and 10. Then ask: **How can we lovingly deal with people like Diotrephes?** (Call attention to the things they're doing. Confront them according to biblical guidelines.)

Jude—Love builds us up and sustains us (20, 21). God's love upholds and cleanses us (24, 25).

Have someone read Jude 11-13. Say: **This is not friendly talk. These are fighting words. How can this be Christian love?** Refer back to the first roleplay at the beginning of the session. Point out that the people described in Jude 11-13 are kind of like the person in the roleplay at the beginning of the session who was trying to convince another person to jump out of the airplane with no parachute. It does not go against the principles of Christian love to point out—in as strong terms as necessary—the dangerous errors in the words of false teachers (or people who are giving bad advice).

STEP 4

What Would You Do?

Have group members remain in the teams they formed in Step 3. Assign each team one of the following case studies. Give each team a few minutes to discuss its situation and come up with the best possible solution (based on the "love principles" found in the epistles you covered in this session). Then have each team share its solution with the rest of the group.

The case studies are as follows. Use the information in parentheses to supplement the teams' responses.

***Case Study #1*—Your friend Marcie has a boyfriend who's trying to talk her into using cocaine with him. She's unsure about what to do. She's scared of using cocaine, but she's also afraid of losing her boyfriend. She tells you about her feelings. How would you show Christian love to Marcie?** (Out of concern for Marcie's health, the first step would be to adamantly encourage her not to use cocaine. The second, and more difficult, step would be to convince her that her boyfriend really doesn't care for her if he wants her to do something as dangerous as taking cocaine. If Marcie then dumps her boyfriend, you could show her Christian love by spending time with her and reassuring her that she made the right decision.)

***Case Study #2*—Your friend Ray has been partying late all weekend, while you stayed home and worked on a paper for history class. Now it's Sunday night, the paper's due tomorrow, and Ray asks for your help with his paper. How would you show Christian love to Ray?** (As tough as it may sound, Christian love sometimes involves allowing people to suffer the consequences of their actions. If you have time, you might answer some of Ray's questions about the assignment; but you shouldn't give him any help that might be construed as cheating.)

***Case Study #3*—Your friend Christy has been reading a book that says Jesus faked His own death and traveled to India. It goes on to say that all religions are basically the same, that Jesus would agree with Buddha, Muhammad, and others. The important thing, the book says, is to be happy in what you believe and to be nice to others. Christy has been telling other kids in the youth group about this, and some of them have bought the book. How would you show Christian love in this situation?** (In a sense, Christy is acting as a "false teacher," spreading untrue doctrines about Christ. Both your love for God and your love for Christy dictate that you confront her about the book. To not do so would mean allowing Christy and other kids to believe blasphemous teachings—a belief that could have eternal implications for Christy and the others.)

***Case Study #4*—You're walking with some of your friends at school when you pass Ernie, who's handing out Christian tracts in the hallway. Your friends start making fun of Ernie—who, by the way, is a pretty obnoxious guy. How would you show Christian love in this situation?** (You might stick up for Ernie in front of your friends, letting them know that you're a Christian and aren't ashamed of the Gospel. Then, later, you might talk with Ernie privately and lovingly explain to him how he's being perceived by other people in the school.)

Before you close the session in prayer, ask group members to think of a situation in their lives in which they can demonstrate their faith by courageously showing love to someone. This might involve confrontation, encouragement, or something else. Give group members a minute or two to pray about their situations. Then close the prayer time by asking God to give group members the courage to do what they need to do in the complex situations of their lives.

OPTIONS

General Letters: FACT SHEET

HEBREWS
Author: We don't know—possibly Paul, Apollos, or Barnabas.
Themes: Christ is all we need to be reconciled with God. All other methods for being reconciled with God—including the priests and sacrifices of the Jewish faith—are obsolete, now that Christ has come.
Key Passages: Hebrews 1:1-3; 4:15, 16; 12:1-3

JAMES
Author: James, brother of Jesus and leader of the early church
Themes: Faith in tough times, the importance of good deeds (especially to the poor)
Key Passages: James 1:17, 22; 4:7

I PETER
Author: Peter, disciple of Jesus and leader of the early church
Themes: Holiness, submission to authorities, enduring persecution
Key Passages: I Peter 1:15, 16; 2:9; 3:15, 16; 5:7

II PETER
Author: Peter, disciple of Jesus and leader of the early church
Themes: Christian growth, the need to oppose false teachers, the Lord's return
Key Passages: II Peter 1:20, 21; 3:8, 9

I JOHN
Author: John, disciple of Jesus and leader of the early church
Themes: Exposing false teachers, assurance of salvation
Key Passages: I John 1:5-9; 3:16, 17; 4:10, 19

II & III JOHN
Author: John, disciple of Jesus and leader of the early church
Themes: Exposing false teachers, imitating what is good rather than what is evil
Key Passages: II John 6; III John 11

JUDE
Author: Jude, probably another brother of Jesus
Theme: Perseverance against false teachers
Key Passages: Jude 20, 21, 24, 25

THE VISITOR

ANN *(singing, while brushing her hair at a mirror)*: "I feel pretty, oh, so pretty—"
JAMES *(stepping in suddenly)*: Excuse me, are you Ann Abernathy?
ANN *(surprised)*: Who are you? What are you doing here?
JAMES: Hi, I'm James, brother of Jesus. You may have read my letter.
ANN: Your letter? I didn't get any—
JAMES: It's in the Bible. *(Scans an imaginary bookshelf, pulls out a Bible, and blows dust off it.)* Here. See?
ANN *(still unsure)*: OK.
JAMES: We're trying a new thing these days. God is sending us down to do preliminary entrance exams for heaven. It's a trial program, and you're one of the lucky test cases.
ANN: You mean my time is up? But I'm so young.
JAMES: Oh, no! You have about fifty years left. Let's see . . . *(checks clipboard)* you die in 2047. World War 5. Oops, I wasn't supposed to tell you that. Anyway, I need to ask you a few questions.
ANN: Well, fire away.
JAMES: Fire? That's the other guys. Ha, ha. Just a little afterlife joke there. So, Miss Abernathy, what makes you think you should go to heaven?
ANN: I believe in Jesus. *(Pause)* That's right, isn't it?
JAMES: Well, yes, but—
ANN: More specific information, I know. I believe in Jesus Christ, Son of God, who died for my sins and rose the third day.
JAMES: OK. Prove it.
ANN: What do you mean?
JAMES: How do I know you're not just saying that?
ANN: I said it! Why would I say it if I didn't believe it? I believe in Jesus. Isn't that enough?
JAMES: Ann, if you go to hell—
ANN: What?!!
JAMES: Let me finish. If you go to hell right now, you'll find a pack of demons who "believe" in Jesus. They know who He is and what He did. And they're terrified of Him—scared to death, so to speak. What makes you any different?
ANN: Look, James, I have faith. That's all I need. *(Looking up to heaven)* Could you send Paul down here? I'm sure he'll straighten this out.
JAMES: I've been doing some research, Ann. Last week at school, you were hanging with the girls—the power patrol—and they were making fun of Cheryl Ann Woodley, with the thick glasses and the bad wardrobe. Remember? Seems to me that faith would have made you stand up for the poor kid. But no, you joined right in.
ANN: You don't understand. I'm trying to get those girls to come to church. And then we'll have a lot of cool kids in the youth group, and we'll get other cool kids and—
JAMES: Church, smurch! I'm not talking about church. I'm talking about Jesus Christ making a difference in your life. Jesus was standing there with Cheryl Ann Woodley and you didn't even see Him. As I recall, you were saying something about . . . *(checks clipboard)* "the K-Mart clearance rack."
ANN: So I goofed. But I'm forgiven, right?
JAMES: If you want to be. But when have you ever done anything for someone that you couldn't get something back from? From what I can see, your Christianity is all in your head. It needs to be in your life. You believe a bunch of facts about Jesus, but you need to give your life to Him. *(Checks watch)* Hey, my time is up—but yours isn't. *(He exits.)*
ANN *(turning back to mirror, depressed)*: "I feel gritty, oh, so gritty . . ."

EXTRA ACTION

Step 1
Have kids form three teams. Give one team a golf club, one a baseball bat, and one a tennis racket. Have each team prepare to demonstrate to the others how to use its piece of sports equipment properly. The catch is that each person on a team must come up with a different way to use that team's equipment. One person on the team should prepare to demonstrate the correct form; the rest should come up with swings and stances that may *seem* right, but aren't. After a few minutes, have the teams demonstrate their equipment. After each team's demonstration, the rest of the group will vote (using a secret ballot) on whose form was correct. The team that's best at fooling the others—that is, the team inspiring the most incorrect guesses—wins. Explain that many of the epistles you'll be studying were designed to instruct "amateurs" in how to live the Christian life, amid the confusion caused by false teachers.

Step 2
Instead of using the skit on Repro Resource 8, try another option. Have kids stand in the middle the room, arm's length apart. Then read the following instructions: (1) **If you believe in God, take a step forward.** (2) **If you believe Jesus is the only way to heaven, take a step to the left.** (3) **If you believe Jesus will return someday, take a step to the right.** (4) **If you believe the Bible is God's Word, take a step back.** (5) **If you believe Jesus rose from the dead, take a step to the right.** (6) **If you believe Jesus loves you, take a step to the left.** If kids took all of these "steps of faith," they should be back where they started. Point out that simply believing facts about Jesus doesn't get us anywhere. Only acting on those beliefs by surrendering to Him—a step those "believing" demons in James 2:19 won't take—will save us.

SMALL GROUP

Step 2
Using the tiles from two or more Scrabble games, find the letters for the titles of the eight non-Pauline epistles. Mix the letters together and place them in the middle of a table. Have your kids take turns trying to unscramble the titles. Time each contestant and write his or her results on the board. Kids may not consult their Bibles while unscrambling the words, so it will be necessary for them to try to memorize the eight titles while other people are competing. Award a prize to the person who correctly unscrambles the words in the shortest amount of time.

Step 4
Kids are more likely to share personal anecdotes in a small group than they are in a large one. With this in mind, try to personalize the closing activity for your group members. Ask each person to share either (1) a situation in which he or she was able to show Christian love to someone else or (2) a situation in which someone showed Christian love to him or her. To "break the ice" for this activity, share an example or two from your own life. Discuss each person's anecdote by asking one of the following questions: **How did you feel after you showed love to the person? How did you feel after the person showed love to you?**

LARGE GROUP

Step 3
Have kids form six groups. Assign one of the following books from Repro Resource 7 to each group: I Peter, II Peter, I John, II John, III John, and Jude. (Obviously, the groups assigned II John and III John will have less material to work with than the other groups do, but they still should have enough.) Instruct each small group to come up with a memorable way to present its book (and the relevant information about the book) to the rest of the group. For instance, for I Peter, group members might stagger to the front of the room, pretending to be injured, to indicate that I Peter was written to people who were facing persecution. Other groups may use cheers, poems, skits, puns, etc. to present their books. After all of the books have been presented, have the group vote on which presentation was most memorable. Award prizes to the winning group.

Step 4
Have kids form four teams. Assign each team one of the case studies. Instruct each team to come up with the best possible solution for its assigned situation. Then, rather than just explaining the solution to the rest of the group, have the team create a roleplay that explains the situation and incorporates the team's solution. After a few minutes, have each team present its roleplay. When each team is finished performing, give the rest of the group members an opportunity to offer alternative solutions for the situation. If they can come up with a better solution, the team must act it out.

OPTIONS

S E S S I O N F O U R

Step 2
The word *faith* may have lost its meaning to your kids. As a group, come up with a new word to take its place—a made-up word that sums up what faith is. (Examples might include *futuremachine* or *invisibridge* [a way to get to a place we can't see yet]; *Godgrip* or *Lordlean* [depending on God]; *toughknowing* or *heartstrength* [a quality that's more than just mental].) Use your made-up word in place of the word *faith*.
In Step 3, the word *love* may have lost its meaning as well—except in a romantic context. Bring some traditional "sweet-heart" gifts—box of candy, flowers, etc. Also post newspaper photos of people in need (famine victims, neglected children, crime victims, etc.). Ask: **Which gifts would you send to which people to express your love for them? Can you think of more appropriate gifts?** Discuss practical ways to show love to needy people, reminding kids that fellow group members have needs too.

Step 4
If the first two case studies seem like clichés, try the following ones instead.
• **You're picketing outside an abortion clinic. A pregnant girl gets out of a car and tries to enter the clinic. Other demonstrators are shouting at her and holding up pictures of aborted fetuses. The girl is crying and scared, but determined to go into the clinic. How do you show Christian love?**
• **You've just gotten an English essay back from the teacher. You usually get good grades, but this paper is marked with a "D." You tried to share your faith in the essay, and thought you did a good job. The teacher's note says, "This is not a religion class. These pat answers are unworthy of you. Next time use your head, not your Bible." How do you show Christian love?**

Step 1
Before the session, hide several coins around the room. When kids arrive, say: **Today's your lucky day. You're sitting on a "gold mine." But no one's going to give you the gold. You have to look for it.** Explain that there are several coins hidden in the room. Give kids about five minutes to search. Afterward, have kids share how much they found. Point out that if they hadn't known any valuables were in the room, they would never have looked for them. The same is true for parts of Scripture—the non-Pauline letters, for example. Many people don't know what's in these eight books near the end of the Bible. That's unfortunate, because they contain many valuable things—explanations of what faith is, tips for loving others, etc. These "valuables" just have to be "searched out."

Step 3
As kids toss out ideas of what comes to mind when they think of *love*, write their responses on the board. After you've listed several ideas, say: **I didn't hear anyone mention things like parents punishing their kids. Don't parents always say, "I'm doing this because I love you"? Come on! Do you believe that?** Get a couple of responses. Then point out that this "tough love" concept also applies to Christianity. Christians are instructed to "sharpen" and "build up" each other. Sometimes this involves conflict or saying things that someone else may not want to hear. It may not *seem* very loving, but it is. Use this discussion to introduce the case studies in Step 4.

Step 3
Lead your group members in singing a couple of hymns and/or choruses that are based on passages or themes from the non-Pauline epistles. Among the hymns and choruses you might consider using are "Great Is Thy Faithfulness" and "And Can It Be That I Should Gain."

Step 4
As you wrap up the session, focus your kids' attention on the first seven words of Hebrews 10:25: "Let us not give up meeting together." Ask: **On a scale of one to ten—with ten being the highest—how important would you say this group is to you?** Encourage kids to respond honestly. **What are some things that might cause us to give up meeting together?** (Boredom, other priorities, kids moving away, "outgrowing" each other, etc.) Unroll a large sheet of paper. Have plenty of colored markers (or perhaps paint and paintbrushes) available. As a group, create a banner with the words of Hebrews 10:25 on it. Hang it in your room as a reminder of the biblical emphasis placed on meeting togther. Encourage your kids to make the group a priority in their lives.

MOSTLY GIRLS

Step 2

Lest your girls think that only men are included in the "Faith Hall of Fame" in Hebrews 11, include verse 31, which talks about Rahab, a woman who risked her life for God's work and was saved because of it. If your girls aren't familiar with Rahab's story, read Joshua 2:1-24; 6:25. Ask: **Why do you think a prostitute would be included on a list with some of the greatest people of faith such as Noah, Abraham, and Moses? What does that say to you and me?** (That God can do great things through us, even if society doesn't see us as someone "great.") **Is that an encouragement to you? Why or why not?**

Step 4

Substitute the following for Case Study #2 in the session:

- ***Case Study #2*—Your friend Lisa has a problem with shoplifting. You're with her and some other friends at the mall, and you see her drop a pair of earrings into her purse. She's not one of your closest friends, but she's part of the group. If you reject one part of the group, it's like you're rejecting them all. How do you show Christian love in this situation?**

MOSTLY GUYS

Step 2

For guys who enjoy living "in the fast lane," the idea that sin can "entangle" us or slow us down has very little relevance. You might want to use a relay race as an object lesson. Have kids form two teams. Make sure that the teams are fairly even in terms of the athleticism of their members. Explain that the teams will be competing in a simple relay race. Designate a race course. (One that included a stair climb would be ideal.) But just before you start the race, announce that the members of one team will have to carry something while they run. Bring out some kind of heavy object—perhaps a king-size box of laundry detergent, a large bag of potatoes, etc.—for the team to carry. Start the race. Unless something odd occurs, the "unhindered" team will probably win the race easily. After the race is over, have your guys look at Hebrews 12:1-3.

Step 4

Add one more case study for your guys to discuss—one that is likely to provoke a little more discussion than the other four:

- ***Case Study #5*—Your best friend Tony is the star of the junior high football team. However, the coach of the high school team and some of the high school players have told Tony that he'll have to "bulk up" if he wants to play high school ball next year. A couple of the high school players told Tony about a guy at a local health club who sold illegal steroids. They said the steroids would bulk Tony up in no time. More than anything in the world, Tony wants to play high school—and, eventually college—football. So he started taking the steroids. How would you show Christian love to Tony?**

EXTRA FUN

Step 1

Blindfold three or four volunteers. Place a large bowl on a table in front of them. Pour a jumbo-size jar of Prego spaghetti sauce—the kind with six vegetables in it—into the bowl. Instruct volunteers to put their hands in the bowl to see if they can identify what's in it. Probably all will be able to identify the spaghetti sauce because of the smell. Take off the blindfolds (and let the volunteers wash their hands). Say: **It *was* spaghetti sauce—but did you know what was in it?** Explain that the sauce contained several vegetables. Have the volunteers, one at a time, go back to the bowl to try to find a vegetable. When they find one, have them hold it up and say (in their best Prego-TV-commercial voice), "It's in there." Afterward, point out that the non-Pauline letters are kind of like the spaghetti sauce. Most people know they're part of the Bible; but many don't really know what's "in there." Explain that there's a lot of good, healthy stuff for us in these books—just like there's a lot of good stuff in spaghetti sauce.

Step 2

Before you go through Repro Resource 7, use the information on the sheet for a quiz to see how much your kids already know about these eight books of the Bible. Have kids form teams. Explain that you will read information on or a passage from one of the eight non-Pauline letters. (Write the titles of the books on the board.) Teams will then guess which book it is. A correct guess is worth one point; an incorrect guess is worth minus-one point (so kids won't just randomly shout out answers). Because kids probably know little about these books, this quiz is strictly for fun. However, at the end of the step, you might want to conduct the quiz again and see how much kids remember.

MEDIA

Step 2
During the week before the session, videotape clips from several shows on Christian TV. Most of these probably will feature talking or singing. At this point in the meeting, show the tape. Ask: **Why do you think there's so much talking and singing on Christian TV? Why don't we see things like dramas and situation comedies, and more of life outside a studio?** You may want to point out that it's partly for financial reasons. Talk shows and musical programs are cheaper to produce than dramas, comedies, or documentaries. But it may also be because talking and singing are what many Christians do best. For many believers, the Christian life seems to revolve around words, not actions. Ask: **How could this relate to faith and works?** As needed, point out that we need to act out our faith in the "real" world, not just talk about it.

Step 4
During the week or two before this meeting, take slides or videos of group members, and of the group having fun together (or collect slides or videos you've taken already). Show the pictures to conclude this session, having kids sing "We Are One in the Spirit" as the images are shown. Call special attention to the phrase "and they'll know we are Christians by our love." Ask: **What's one thing you could do this month to strengthen the bond of love in our group? How can the rest of us help you do that?**

SHORT MEETING TIME

Step 1
Skip Step 1. Start with Repro Resource 7. Assign each epistle to a different person or team (doubling up as needed). As each person gets a "taste" of an epistle, let him or her also taste a food that corresponds to his or her book. Here are some suggestions: "Jewish" food (like matzohs) for Hebrews; "poor people's" food (like canned beans) for James; "endurance" food (like Gatorade) for I Peter; "growth" food (like strained carrots for babies) for II Peter; "love" food (like chocolates) for I John; "false" food (like imitation crabmeat) for II and III John; "rescue" food (like Ultra Slim-Fast) for Jude. As kids share the results of their studies, have them explain how their foods related to their epistles. After discussing James, have kids perform the skit on Repro Resource 8. Skip most of the rest of Steps 2 and 3, except for the discussion at the end of Step 3 on what can be learned about love from the epistles.

Step 4
Instead of using all of the case studies in Step 4, use just Case Study #3. Have the whole group discuss it. In the process of discussion, however, inject the "faith and works" issue as well. Say: **Christy's book says that all people who have tried to live good lives will go to heaven. Using what James says about faith and works, what could you tell Christy? What if Christy replies that she hasn't seen you doing many good works lately, so your faith must be dead? How could you answer in a way that's loving and honest?**

URBAN

Step 2
Have the two teams (the "Hebrews Team" and the "James Team") participate in a three-part competition. The premise of the competition is to see which team can make its book seem more appealing to an urban audience. You will serve as judge for the competition. For the first contest, give the teams three minutes to come up with a skit based on a passage from their book. The Hebrews Team will base its skit on Hebrews 1:1-3; the James Team will base its skit on James 1:17. Award one point to the team that comes up with the most original skit. For the second contest, give the teams three minutes to come up with a song based on a passage from their book. The Hebrews Team will base its song on Hebrews 4:15, 16; the James Team will base its song on James 1:22. Award one point to the team that comes up with the most original song. For the third contest, give the teams three minutes to come up with a game based on a passage from their book. The Hebrews Team will base its game on Hebrews 12:1-3; the James Team will base its game on James 1:17. Award one point to the team that comes up with the most original game. You might want to give prizes to the team that wins the most points.

Step 3
Before you focus on the love we should show to others, spend some time talking about the love God shows us. Explain that God's love is a "tough love." It's not a return affection for our love for Him; God loves us regardless of how we feel about Him. As a group, brainstorm examples of how God has shown (or still shows) love to us when we don't deserve it. Then, if you have time at the end of the session, create some T-shirt logos illustrating God's love for us.

JR. HIGH / HIGH SCHOOL COMBINED

Step 3
Have your junior highers and high schoolers compete in a "mnemonics" contest. Give each group seven pieces of poster board and markers. See which group can create the best mnemonic (memory-aiding) picture for each book (or group of books) on Repro Resource 7. Each picture should convey as much information as possible. Kids may not use words in their pictures; the only numbers they may use are the references for key passages. Give the groups several minutes to work. When they're finished, have each one present and explain its picture for each book. You'll judge which picture is best for each book and award a point to that group. The group with the most points at the end of the game is the winner.

Step 4
After completing the case studies, have your junior highers and high schoolers (each working as a separate group) think of the *one* situation in which it would be hardest for them to show Christian love for someone else. The two groups will be competing to see who can come up with the more difficult situation. After a few minutes, have each group share its situation. Then give each group an opportunity to suggest solutions for the other group's situation—thereby proving that *its* situation was more difficult. After listening to the groups' solutions, you will decide whose situation was harder.

SIXTH GRADE

Step 3
As a group, come up with a simple phrase (no more than three or four words) to summarize the information about each book (or group of books) on Repro Resource 7. For instance, you might use "Christ—all we need" for Hebrews; "faith and deeds" for James; etc. Write the phrases on the board as you come up with them. Then give group members an opportunity to memorize the phrases. After a few minutes, erase or cover up the phrases. Then have each of your group members see how many phrases he or she can recall. You might want to award a prize to the person who can recite the most. Throughout the rest of the session, randomly "test" your kids to see how many phrases they still recall (e.g., **Sonya, what's the phrase for I John?**).

Step 4
Substitute the following case studies for your sixth graders:
• ***Case Study #1*—Your friend Jeff doesn't play sports like most other guys at school. Instead, he prefers reading and playing music. He's a trained pianist and plays flute in the school band. Most of the other guys at school make fun of Jeff, calling him names like "sissy" and "Jeffanie"—and worse. They say that anyone who hangs around with Jeff must be "like" him, if you know what I mean. How would you show Christian love to Jeff?**
• ***Case Study #2*—As a joke, your friend Alicia hid Michelle's purse in a dumpster behind the school. Michelle told the teacher that someone stole her purse. Now the teacher and the principal are interviewing students one by one, trying to find out what happened. You're the only person who knows what Michelle did. Michelle, afraid of getting in trouble, begs you not to tell. How could you show Christian love to Michelle?**

PLANNING CHECKLIST

Date Used:

Approx. Time

Step 1: Roleplay Mania ______
o Extra Action
o Little Bible Background
o Extra Fun
o Short Meeting Time

Step 2: Faith: The Facts ______
o Extra Action
o Small Group
o Heard It All Before
o Mostly Girls
o Mostly Guys
o Extra Fun
o Media
o Urban

Step 3: Love, Biblical Style ______
o Large Group
o Little Bible Background
o Fellowship & Worship
o Urban
o Combined Jr. High/High School
o Sixth Grade

Step 4: What Would You Do? ______
o Small Group
o Large Group
o Heard It All Before
o Fellowship & Worship
o Mostly Girls
o Mostly Guys
o Media
o Short Meeting Time
o Combined Jr. High/High School
o Sixth Grade

SESSION

5 And in the End . . . (Revelation)

YOUR GOALS FOR THIS SESSION:

Choose one or more

☐ To help kids become familiar with the Book of Revelation.

☐ To help kids understand the key principles of worship and God's ultimate victory.

☐ To encourage kids to live in the confidence of Christ's victory.

☐ Other ______________________________
____

Your Bible Base:

Selected passages from Revelation

STEP 1

The Fix Is In

(Needed: A note card, prepared according to instructions)

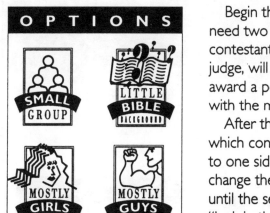

OPTIONS

Begin the session with a game to test contestants' creativity. You'll need two contestants—a guy and a girl. In each round, you'll ask the contestants to name something in a particular category. You, as the judge, will determine which of their answers is more "creative" and award a point to that person. (Your decision is final.) The contestant with the most points after nine rounds is the winner.

After three rounds, the rest of the group members will "vote" on which contestant they think will win the game. They will vote by moving to one side of the room or the other. Throughout the contest, they may change their votes and switch sides of the room as often as they like—until the seventh round. After the seventh round, group members must "lock in their votes" and stay on one side of the room.

What your contestants won't know is that the game is fixed. The guy will win the first four rounds; the girl will win the last five rounds (and, ultimately, the game).

Before the game, you'll need to prepare a note card that reads, "The girl will win the game. Don't tell anyone, but pass this card to someone else." As the game begins, secretly hand the card to a group member.

Here are some categories you can use:

1. **Name a kind of food.** (Guy wins.)
2. **Name a TV show.** (Guy wins.)
3. **Name a kind of car.** (Guy wins.)
4. **Name a holiday.** (Guy wins.)
5. **Name a color.** (Girl wins.)
6. **Name a style of music.** (Girl wins.)
7. **Name a sport.** (Girl wins.)
8. **Name a household appliance.** (Girl wins.)
9. **Name a brand of cereal.** (Girl wins.)

When the game is over, congratulate your winner. Then have the rest of the group members explain why they voted as they did.

Ask those who voted for the girl: **Why did you vote for her? Did the card influence your decision? Did it look bleak there for a while when the guy was ahead 4-0? What made you stay with her?**

Ask those who voted for the guy: **Why did you vote for him? Did any of you see the card? If so, why didn't you believe it?**

Afterward, use the activity to introduce the session topic. Say: **For Christians, there are times in our lives—and times in history—when it seems God's side is losing. But the message of the Bible—and especially the Book of Revelation—is that God and His side will win in the end. The Book of Revelation is the card that is passed from person to person throughout the centuries that says, "Christ will win. Pass it on."**

STEP 2

Special Delivery

(Needed: Bibles, copies of Repro Resource 9, pencils)

Hand out copies of "Report Card: The Seven Churches" (Repro Resource 9) and pencils. Explain: **The beginning of Revelation is a series of short letters that Jesus dictated to John. These letters were addressed to seven churches in Asia Minor—an area that is now Turkey. But we can also see characteristics of such churches even now.**

Have group members form pairs. Assign one or more (depending on the size of your group) of the seven churches to each pair. Instruct each pair to read its assigned passage, assign a letter grade (A, B, C, D, or F) to the church based on how well it's doing, write down the positive and negative things mentioned about the church, and write down any similarities between the church mentioned in the letter and some modern-day churches.

Give the pairs a few minutes to work. When they're finished, have each one share its findings. Use the following information to supplement the pairs' responses.

Ephesus (Revelation 2:1-7)—Positives might include things like hard work, perseverance, and the willingness to test people who claimed to be apostles. The primary negative aspect of the church is that it had forsaken "its first love." Perhaps their love for each other and/or Christ had drifted away as they became more suspicious and perhaps legalistic. There are many churches like this today—solid in doctrine, but lacking in love.

Smyrna (Revelation 2:8-11)—One positive aspect of the church is that it withstood persecution. There are no real negatives mentioned. This is a comforting, strengthening letter. Modern counterparts to this church might be persecuted churches in countries like China or Egypt.

Pergamum (Revelation 2:12-17)—One positive aspect of the church is that it had remained true in the midst of trial. One negative aspect is that it tolerated false teachers, who may have been urging church members to compromise with the world. Even today, some churches seem to support the teaching of moral laxity.

Thyatira (Revelation 2:18-29)—Positives might include things like love, faith, service, and perseverance. One negative aspect is that the church tolerated "Jezebel," who seduced people into sexual immorality and idol worship. Modern counterparts to this church might include the "show-biz" churches that buy into media seduction without realizing its danger.

Sardis (Revelation 3:1-6)—Positives might include some good deeds, a good reputation, and a few pure people. Negatives might include lethargy and deadness. There are many such "ho-hum" churches today.

Philadelphia (Revelation 3:7-13)—Positives might include the Phillies (just kidding) and faithful endurance—even with little strength. There are no negatives mentioned about the church. Modern counterparts might include faithful congregations in very poor areas of the world like Zaire and Haiti.

Laodicea (Revelation 3:14-22)—About the only positive thing mentioned is that Jesus loves those whom He rebukes. And the Laodiceans were certainly being rebuked! Negatives might include a lukewarmness, an arrogant affluence, and an ignorance of their need. There are many churches today that are proud of themselves ("fat and happy") when they actually need major healing from the Lord.

After you've covered the seven churches, say: **Some people think of Revelation as a mystical, spooky vision of the end times. You've probably already noticed the strange visual language—the seven stars, the double-edged sword, and so on. That's part of the literary style of the book. But we have to remember that there's a purpose to this language. This book was written to seven churches on the "cutting edge." They had specific problems, from within and without. They had specific needs. And the first thing they needed was a vision of the greatness of God.**

STEP 3

Weird Worship

(Needed: Bibles, copies of Repro Resource 9, pencils)

Have group members remain in the pairs they formed in Step 2. Assign one or more of the following passages to each pair: Revelation 4:7-11; 5:6-10; 5:11-14; 7:9-12; 11:15-18; 15:1-4; and 19:1-5. Instruct the pairs to read their assigned passage(s) and then answer the questions at the bottom of Repro Resource 9. After a few minutes, have each pair share its responses.

Then say: **It seems like every time you turn a page in Revelation, there's a worship service going on. It's like you're in the middle of a Star Trek convention—creatures with wings and eyes and faces of animals. And they're always singing praises. Beasts and elders and angels and multitudes all bow in worship to God. And what do they praise God for? His holiness, His worthiness, His power, His mighty acts for His people, His victory, His future reign, and so on. God is great!**

How do you think people in the faithful churches—like Smyrna and Philadelphia—would feel when they read this? (Perhaps pumped up or encouraged.)

How do you think people in the lazy or corrupted churches—like Laodicea—would feel? (Perhaps challenged or awakened.)

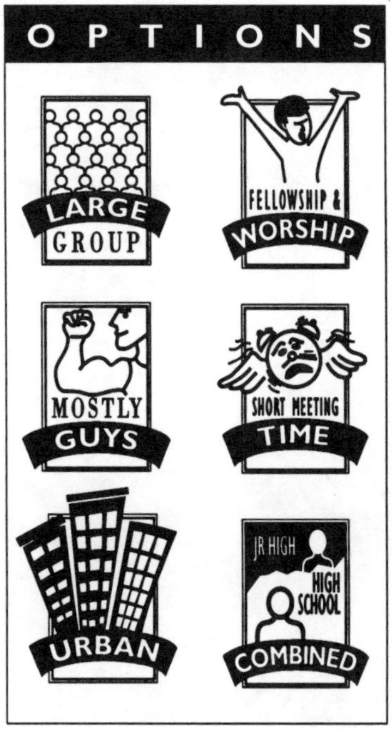

STEP 4

Making Sense of the End Times

(Needed: Copies of Repro Resource 10, chalkboard and chalk or newsprint and marker)

Explain: **The middle section of Revelation focuses on the battle against the Lord, and how the Lord deals with it. And**

OPTIONS

once again we find figurative language. You may want to write some of the following information on the board as you mention it.

There are seven "seals" of judgment. Think of these as sealed envelopes that are opened one by one to reveal war, famine, plague, on so on. There are seven "trumpets" that announce other disasters. There are two "witnesses" who testify for the Lord, but are killed by God's enemies. There are 144,000 faithful people whom God protects. We also find a dragon, a couple of other beasts, and a prostitute—all opposed to the Lord. There are seven "bowls" of God's wrath poured out on the rebellious world, leading to a great battle at Armageddon. And there is the Lamb—obviously a symbol of Christ—who emerges victorious.

Because the language of this text is so fanciful, many different theories have been developed on how to put it all together. Unfortunately, sometimes people can get so wrapped up in their theories that they miss the obvious point.

Ask for two volunteers to perform a brief skit. Hand each of them a copy of "The End of the World As We Know It" (Repro Resource 10). Give the actors a minute or two to read through the script. Then have them perform the skit.

Afterward, ask: **Is it wrong to try to figure out the details of the end times? How do you feel about the attitude of the person who was excited in the skit?** (The end times seemed to be a game to him or her. He or she was trying to fit the pieces together and, as a result, behaved totally inappropriately in the face of human disasters.)

When people talk about Armageddon or bar codes, they seem to be trying to instill fear. How does this compare with the purpose of Revelation? (Revelation was a reassurance to the faithful believers that God was in control. It might instill a godly fear in the hearts of unbelievers, but it should comfort Christians.)

The other person in the skit said he (or she) was trying to make this world better. Is there any value in that outlook? (Yes and no. We need to be sharing our Christianity in every way we can, helping people in need, working for what's right, and telling people the good news. That may make things better. But we must be prepared for society to rebel against God. The world may be getting worse, but we still need to serve God here.)

Explain that there are four major theories about how we should view the Book of Revelation. Write the theories on the board as you talk about them.

1. That Was Then. Some people believe that Revelation refers to events that were going on in the time of John (who probably wrote it in the 90s A.D.). The Roman Empire had unleashed a major persecution against Christians. Some say the book figuratively describes Christian opposition and God's ultimate victory.

2. *Every Age.* Some people say that Revelation describes ongoing opposition to God, and God's ongoing victory over evil. In every age, opponents rise up against the Lord, and in every age God redeems the faithful.

3. *Future General.* Some people say that Revelation describes future events, but in a general way. They say that attempts to identify this beast or that army are doomed to fail. The point is that God will ultimately triumph over evil at some future time.

4. *Future Specific.* Some people say that the fanciful language of John describes specific events that will happen, or are happening. This is allegory, they say, in which each thing stands for something real. Within this theory, there are several different ideas of how to interpret the details.

If your church feels strongly about any particular theory, you may want to share that briefly here. But don't overwhelm the main point—that God will win this "game." Sometimes it may seem that He's behind on the scoreboard, but He will win. We can count on it.

STEP 5

Final Victory

(Needed: Bibles, copies of Repro Resource 9, pencils)

Have group members turn to Revelation 21. Explain that the Book of Revelation ends with a beautiful picture of our eternal life with God, the aftermath of God's mighty victory.

Have someone read Revelation 21:1-4. Then ask: **How does this make you feel?** Get a few responses.

Then get kids thinking about their own lives. Ask: **Are you like one of the churches we talked about earlier? Are you kind of dead in your faith? Do you need a wake-up call? Are you satisfied when you shouldn't be? Have you forgotten how to love? Do you feel burdened by the opposition you get from other people? Do you need reassurance?**

Remember the message of Revelation: God is great. He will win. We have a bright future ahead of us.

Is there something you need to be doing differently in your life because of these truths? Is there a way you can line up

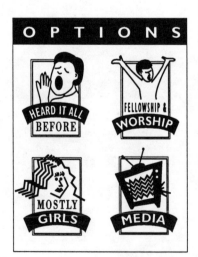

OPTIONS

behind Christ, the winner? Do you need to be bolder in talking about Him? Is there some area of your life in which you could be pleasing Him more?

Ask group members to write on the back of Repro Resource 9 an action step they will take this week. Have them finish this sentence: "Because Christ has won the victory, I will . . ."

When everyone is finished, say: **Christ invites us into a relationship with Him, a relationship to last forever.**

Ask someone to read Revelation 22:17. Then close in prayer, thanking God for the reassurance of His ultimate victory.

REPORT CARD: THE SEVEN CHURCHES

1. Ephesus
(Revelation 2:1-7)

Grade:

Positives:

Negatives:

Similar churches today?

2. Smyrna
(Revelation 2:8-11)

Grade:

Positives:

Negatives:

Similar churches today?

3. Pergamum
(Revelation 2:12-17)

Grade:

Positives:

Negatives:

Similar churches today?

4. Thyatira
(Revelation 2:18-29)

Grade:

Positives:

Negatives:

Similar churches today?

5. Sardis
(Revelation 3:1-6)

Grade:

Positives:

Negatives:

Similar churches today?

6. Philadelphia
(Revelation 3:7-13)

Grade:

Positives:

Negatives:

Similar churches today?

7. Laodicea
(Revelation 3:14-22)

Grade:

Positives:

Negatives:

Similar churches today?

Assigned Text: ______________________________

Who is worshiping? ______________________________

____

What are they worshiping God/Jesus *for?* ______________________________

____

Describe the feeling you get from reading this. ______________________________

____

THE END OF THE WORLD AS WE KNOW IT

A *(looking at a newspaper)***:** Hey, did you see the news today? Flooding in Brazil, earthquakes in Pakistan, civil war in Uganda. Isn't that great?

B: No, I think it's pretty sad, actually.

A: But don't you see? It's prophesied. All of it. Wars and rumors of wars. Flood. Famine. Plague. The seven seals. The bowls of wrath. Jesus is coming back soon, I just know it. Isn't that great?

B: I guess so.

A: It's unbelievable how it's all coming together. Take the Common Market. Isn't that incredible?

B: The European economic community? I've never really gotten that excited about it.

A: But it's the ten toes, don't you see? I know there are a few extra now, but they don't really count. And the Red Chinese have that awesome army just waiting to march across the Euphrates. It's Armageddon time, right?

B: If you say so.

A: And that Soviet thing threw me for a while, 'cause they were going to be Gog and Magog, but then it hit me. If you're looking for the kings of the north, I have two words for you. Two words. Saddam Hussein. Ayatollah.

B: That's three, I think.

A: And can you believe these bar codes? They're on everything now. They're even talking about tattooing them on the back of your hand. Is that the mark of the beast or what? Need I say more?

B: Not if you don't want to.

A: Society is just going down, down, down. Just like it says in the Bible. The latter days are here, my friend. The world is just going to get worse and worse. Isn't that great?

B: And here I was trying to make it better!

A: Better? Oh, that's a good one. *(Laughs as he exits.)*

EXTRA ACTION

Step 2
Bring a bottle of inexpensive cologne; a jar of chopped, fresh garlic; seven paper cups; and plastic spoons. Give each pair a paper cup and a plastic spoon. Put the cologne and garlic at the front of the room. Instead of giving the seven churches letter grades, each pair should put amounts of cologne and/or garlic into its cup to indicate how its church may have "smelled" to the Lord. (For example, Philadelphia might be all cologne; Laodicea might be all garlic; the others would be various mixtures.) When reports are given, pass around the cups so that everyone can take a whiff. In Step 3, after describing how we'll someday praise God in heaven, play a recording of the "Hallelujah Chorus" from Handel's *Messiah*. Depending on the temperament of your group, have kids either (1) move creatively to express how the music makes them feel; (2) make up a cheerleader-style routine to go with the music; or (3) accompany the music as a percussion section, using pencil "drumsticks" on pie plates, knuckles on tables, etc. Afterward, discuss what it might feel like to praise God face to face.

Step 4
Bring poster board and markers. After (or in place of) the skit on Repro Resource 10, have kids make signs expressing their views of when Christ's return will occur. Some kids may give precise dates. Others may just say "The End Is Near," "Repent," or "Be Prepared." As you summarize the four theories about Revelation, let kids "picket" you by marching around the room with their signs. Then have volunteers explain their signs.

SMALL GROUP

Step 1
It's likely that most of your kids know each other fairly well. Open the session with a trivia quiz based on personal information about your kids. Have kids form two teams. Quietly tell a member of Team #2 that you *guarantee* his or her team will win the game. Have him or her spread the news to the rest of his or her teammates. Ask Team #1 a question (perhaps **Who is the oldest member of your group?**). Team members will confer on their answer. If the team answers correctly, it gets a point. Then ask Team #2 a question. Continue for a few rounds. Try to make sure the teams remain tied throughout the contest. Then announce the beginning of the final round—each team will get one more question. Ask Team #1 a nearly impossible question (like **What is the name of my fourth-grade teacher?**). Ask Team #2 a ridiculously easy question (like **What is the first name of Mark's dad?**—assuming, of course, that Mark is on Team #2). Afterward, explain to the members of the losing team that the game was rigged—they didn't have a chance to win. Then point out that regardless of how things seem now, God's forces will ultimately defeat Satan's forces—Satan doesn't have a chance to win.

Step 2
Go through Repro Resource 9 as a group, assigning letter grades to the seven churches. As you read aloud each of the letters in the Book of Revelation, have your kids assume the roles of people in that church. For instance, for Sardis, some kids might pretend to be sleeping in pews while others talk drowsily about the church's good deeds and good reputation. You don't need to spend a lot of time with this—no more than thirty seconds for each church. Afterward, discuss how these same situations affect churches today.

LARGE GROUP

Step 3
Have kids form seven groups. Assign each group one of the passages listed in the session. Instruct each group to read its passage and then come up with a creative way to present the passage to the rest of the group. For instance, one group member (playing the role of John) may narrate the passage while the rest of the group members act out what the narrator is describing and recite the worship passages in unison. The groups may get as literal as they wish in portraying the various worshiping creatures. (It should be interesting to see their interpretations of six-winged creatures covered with eyes.) After each group finishes, discuss what it felt like to play the part of beings who were worshiping God in such a deep, meaningful way. Ask: **How does our worship compare with what you've just been reading? When you worship, how often do you think about what you're singing or saying to God? How much of your worship is "habit," done without much thought or meaning?**

Step 4
Have kids remain in the seven groups they formed in Step 3 (see the above option). Make sure each group has a copy of a study Bible. Assign each group one of the seven seals (Revelation 6:1–8:5), one of the seven trumpets (8:6–14:20), and one of the seven bowls (15:1–16:21). Instruct each group to find its assigned seal, trumpet, and bowl in the Bible. Then have the group write down what the Bible says will happen during the seal/trumpet/bowl judgments. Encourage the groups to use the notes in the study Bible to help them decipher some of the more confusing passages. After a few minutes, have each group present its findings. Afterward, ask volunteers to share how they feel about the various judgments detailed in the Book of Revelation.

OPTIONS

SESSION FIVE

Step 2
If your kids are interested in only the most bizarre parts of the prophecies of Revelation, they may miss much of what you're trying to get across. Get them to consider their own attitudes by discussing the following *TV Guide* quote from country singer Billy Ray Cyrus: **"I used to watch CNN late at night and document the end of the world with my VCR. . . . I kept a videotape cued up, and every time I saw a story that documented different things from the Book of Revelations in the Bible—wars, earthquakes, the depletion of the ozone layer, world hunger—I'd capture it on tape. . . . I stopped after I saw a story about a bunch of whales that had been slaughtered. I started thinking, 'Man, this is just too sick. . . .' I laugh about it now, but I still watch CNN for those stories. I just don't tape them anymore."** Ask: **Does this sound weird or normal to you? Why? Was Billy Ray Cyrus missing the point of the Book of Revelation? What *is* the point of the book?**

Step 5
The future may seem so distant to kids that they won't feel any urgency about preparing for it. Try the following option to combat this complacency. Before the session, arrange to have a couple of helpers suddenly come crashing into the room, shouting and throwing confetti or shooting Silly String at the group. Their entrance should take place while you're reading Revelation 21:1-4. After your helpers leave, say: **Christ's return could happen any time—by surprise. Any of us could be surprised by sudden death too. Either way, none of us knows how soon we'll stand before God—and how soon Revelation will become the present instead of the future.** Then read Revelation 21:1-4 again and finish the session as written.

Step 1
If your group has little concept of what's in the Bible, the Book of Revelation may be especially tough for them to understand. Begin the session by asking group members to describe how they think the world will end (if indeed they think it *will* end). Some kids may think that a nuclear war will destroy the world. Others may say that the world will end when the sun burns itself out. Still others may say that the world will end when Christ returns. After several kids have responded, explain that the Book of Revelation in the Bible tells us what will happen in the end times. Explain: **The Book of Revelation describes in vivid detail how the world is going to end. Unfortunately, some of the events and images described in the book are pretty confusing. However, one message throughout the book is *crystal clear:* Christians have nothing to fear about the end times. Although it may not always seem that way, God is control of everything.**

Step 4
Kids with little Bible background may be (pleasantly) surprised to learn that something as interesting and action-packed as the seal/trumpet/bowl judgments can be found in the Bible. Have kids form small groups. Give them a few minutes to skim the judgments described in Revelation 6–16. Then have each group come up with an idea for a movie based on the events in the passage. After a few minutes, have each group describe its proposed movie.

Step 3
After you discuss the letter to the church at Smyrna (which is a comforting, strengthening letter), have your kids brainstorm things Christ might say in a letter to your group to provide comfort and strength. For instance, if your group has recently lost a couple of members, Christ's letter might say, "I know your problems and concerns. Do not be downhearted. Though your numbers may be smaller, you still have the ability to accomplish great things. . . ." Write group members' suggestions on the board as they are named. After the session, combine kids' suggestions to create an actual letter (based on the format of the seven letters in the Book of Revelation). Make copies of the letter and pass them out at your next meeting.

Step 5
As you wrap up the session, lead your group members in singing a couple of hymns and/or choruses that are based on passages or themes from the Book of Revelation. Among the hymns and choruses you might consider using are "Onward Christian Soldiers," "When the Roll Is Called Up Yonder," and "All Hail the Power of Jesus' Name."

MOSTLY GIRLS

Step 1
Instead of a guy-girl contest, choose two girls for your contestants. Designate one as Player #1 and the other as Player #2. Player #1 will have the "guy's" role; Player #2 will have the "girl's" role. Player #2 should end up being the winner. The game can be played according to the instructions in the sessions, using the following questions as substitutions:
3. Name a brand of shoes. (Player #1 wins.)
7. Name a brand of perfume. (Player #2 wins.)

Step 5
Challenge your girls to think of a specific problem or need they have right now. Have them take another look at Repro Resource 9 to see if they can identify with one of the churches and its problem. If they're willing to share, ask for volunteers to talk about their problem and how the related Scripture passages could help them deal with it. If they're reluctant to share personal struggles, ask them to think of situations that people their age commonly face and how the related Scripture would apply.

MOSTLY GUYS

Step 1
Begin the session with a tug-of-war contest. Have your guys form two teams. Quietly explain to one of the guys that you plan to help his team win. Have him quietly pass the message to the rest of his teammates. Then have the two teams begin the contest. After a few moments, join in the contest yourself, helping the appropriate team win. Afterward, explain to the losing (and likely complaining) team that their opponents knew that you were going to help them and that they would ultimately win. Then explain that the Book of Revelation details the "tug of war" battle between Satan (and his evil forces) and Christ (and His followers). Point out that sometimes the momentum in the struggle seems to shift back and forth. But ultimately, Christ and His followers are assured victory.

Step 3
Ask: **How many of you guys like to sing?** Get a show of hands. **How many of you like to sing *hymns*?** Ask guys to explain their answers. While some of them may not think twice about singing along with their favorite rock songs, they may think that singing hymns is "boring" or "wimpy." Go through the passages in the session detailing the worship going on in heaven. Then ask: **Why do you think God wants us to worship Him? Are there other ways to worship God besides singing? If so, what are they? How can we prevent the opinions of others—or our own feelings about singing hymns—from interfering with our worship?**

EXTRA FUN

Step 1
Have kids form two teams. Instruct the teams to line up at one end of the room. At the other end, place two bags of food. At your signal, the first person on each team will run to his or her team's bag, pull out a food item, and eat it. After eating it, he or she will run back to the team. Then the next person will continue the process. The first team to finish off its food wins. However, you'll need to rig the contest so that one team wins easily. In the "winning" team's bag, place items that can be eaten quickly—candy bars, Twinkies, etc. In the "losing" team's bag, place items that take a while to eat—Slo-Pokes, jumbo marshmallows, etc. Quietly explain to a member of the "winning" team what you've done. Have the person pass the message to the rest of the team. After the game, explain to the losing team what you did. Then say: **At first, it seemed like the outcome of the game was in doubt. But the team that won *knew* it was going to win.** Point out that the Book of Revelation tells us that God and His side have already won the victory against Satan—even though sometimes it may look like the outcome of the battle is in doubt.

Step 4
Have kids form two groups. Assign each group an area of the room to decorate. One group will decorate for a haunted house, making its area as scary and gloomy as possible. The other group will decorate its area for a party, making its area as festive as possible. You'll need to provide the decoration material. After several minutes, have the teams go through each other's area. Afterward, point out that, similarly, we can take two different attitudes toward the end times. We can be scared and uneasy about them—or we can celebrate them, knowing that God has already won the victory for us.

OPTIONS

SESSION FIVE

Step 1

Adapt the opening activity, using video. During the week before the session, videotape a TV contest—a game show, *American Gladiators*, a pro wrestling match, etc. Instead of asking questions of a guy and girl, play segments of the tape—stopping every so often to take a new vote on who's going to win. Fast-forward the tape as needed after each stop, so that you'll reach the end in five or six "rounds." As in the session's activity, prepare and pass around an index card saying that so-and-so (whoever actually wins) will be the winner. After the winner is revealed, adapt the questions at the end of Step 1 to discuss how the game relates to the Book of Revelation.

Step 5

Play the following songs for your kids. Ask group members which songs come closest to expressing *their* feelings about Revelation, heaven, and the future. The songs are as follows:

- "Eve of Destruction" by Barry McGuire—Things are falling apart; the world's coming to an end.
- "In the Year 2525" by Zager and Evans—Things will probably keep going for a long time, with life on earth getting more and more awful.
- "Heaven Is a Place on Earth" by Belinda Carlisle—This life is all the heaven there is.
- "The Throne" by Michael W. Smith—I'm looking forward to worshiping God.
- "Tears in Heaven" by Eric Clapton—There's a heaven, but I probably don't belong there.

Step 1

Instead of using the activity in the session, try a shorter opening. You'll need a head of lettuce; a bulletin from your church with a large "minus" sign marked on it; a sleeping bag; a paper sack with a "minus" sign on it; a package of hot dogs; and an untrue statement about a group member, written on an index card. Put these objects on a table at the front of the room in no particular order. Say: **Look at these objects. If you arrange them correctly, they form an old saying. Whoever figures it out in one minute gets a prize.** When the minute is up, explain that the saying is "Let sleeping dogs lie" ("lettuce" minus "us" [represented by the bulletin], plus "sleeping bag," minus "bag," plus "dogs," plus "lie" [the untrue statement]). Use this cryptogram as an illustration of the challenge involved in figuring out some of the symbols in the Book of Revelation. In Step 2, have kids study just three representative churches—Ephesus, Pergamum, and Laodicea. If you like, summarize the positives and negatives of the other churches yourself.

Step 3

Switch the order of Steps 3 and 4. Go to Step 4 first, but skip the skit. Then use Step 3, reading just the first three passages listed. In Step 5, read Revelation 21:1-4. Have kids close their eyes as you ask the questions in the third paragraph of Step 5. Follow with thirty seconds of silent prayer in which kids can talk to God about their responses. Then read the fourth paragraph of Step 5 and close in prayer yourself.

Step 2

In addition to (or instead of) having group members evaluate the seven churches listed on Repro Resource 9, give your kids an opportunity to write letters to one or two contemporary urban churches. Briefly compare the situations facing the seven churches described in Revelation with the situations facing contemporary urban churches. Then, as kids write their letters, they should offer encouragement and advice for the churches as the churches face hardship and challenges. (Of course, you'll need to get the addresses of such churches and arrange to mail kids' letters.)

Step 3

As a foretaste of the corporate worship that will occur in heaven, have your group plan a community worship service with one or more other churches and/or youth groups in your area. There are many different themes you could use for such a service. Here are a few ideas to get you started:

- Plan an outdoor "Gospelrama" music fest with several local choirs.
- Plan an evangelical revival service.
- Plan an outdoor worship/"foodfest" for the entire community that involves eating, singing, and preaching.

COMBINED JR. HIGH / HIGH SCHOOL

Step 1
Choose a junior higher and a high schooler to compete in the opening activity. The card you pass around should read, "The junior higher will win the game. Don't tell anyone, but pass this card to someone else." The high schooler will win four rounds; the junior higher will win five (and, ultimately, the game). To make it appear that the high schooler has an advantage, substitute the following categories:
6. Name a high school team nickname. (Junior higher wins.)
9. Name a high school teacher. (Junior higher wins.)
If the junior higher has no clue about high school team nicknames or teachers' names, have him or her throw out a wild guess. Then award him or her the point, explaining that *some* high school *somewhere* has that team nickname or that *some* teacher *somewhere* has that name.

Step 3
Your junior highers may not be able to compete with your high schoolers in contests of skill and speed, but they may be able to hold their own in a "sing-off." Put the two age groups on opposite sides of the room. Your junior highers will go first. Explain that they have five seconds to think of a hymn (like "When Peace Like a River") or chorus (like "Father Abraham") to sing. They must sing the song as a group for ten seconds. Then the high schoolers will have five seconds to think of another song to sing. If a team can't think of a new song to sing within five seconds, the other team wins the round. Play as many rounds as time allows. Award prizes (perhaps kazoos) to the group that wins the most rounds. Use this activity to introduce the topic of singing praises to God in heaven.

SIXTH GRADE

Step 1
Play a video clip or read a newspaper article concerning one of the greatest comebacks in sports history. It occurred in the National Football League. The Buffalo Bills were trailing the Houston Oilers 31-3 at halftime of the 1992 AFC championship game. The Bills came back to win the game. Ask: **If you could go back in time—knowing what you know now—and talk to the Bills in their locker room at halftime, what would you say to them? Do you think they'd believe you? Why or why not? How could you encourage them not to give up?** Point out that, similarly, the Book of Revelation is an encouragement to Christians from someone who knows for sure what's going to happen in the future—God.

Step 4
After briefly listing some of the events described in the middle section of Revelation, say: **This kind of sounds like a movie or a video game, doesn't it?** Have your kids think of movies or video games that contain elements similar to the events described in Revelation. List kids' suggestions on the board as they're named. The list might include things like *Star Wars* and "Dungeons and Dragons." Then say: **I can see how these examples might come to mind, with all of the descriptions of dragons, beasts, and huge battles in Revelation. But a big difference between Revelation and the things on our list is that we already know how Revelation will turn out in the end. You can't know what the final result of a movie or video game will be before you watch or play it. But Revelation gives its ending away—and it's good news for those who love and serve God.**

PLANNING CHECKLIST

Date Used:

Approx. Time

Step 1: The Fix Is In ______
o Small Group
o Little Bible Background
o Mostly Girls
o Mostly Guys
o Extra Fun
o Media
o Short Meeting Time
o Combined Jr. High/High School
o Sixth Grade

Step 2: Special Delivery ______
o Extra Action
o Small Group
o Heard It All Before
o Urban

Step 3: Weird Worship ______
o Large Group
o Fellowship & Worship
o Mostly Guys
o Short Meeting Time
o Urban
o Combined Jr. High/High School

Step 4: Making Sense of the End Times ______
o Extra Action
o Large Group
o Little Bible Background
o Extra Fun
o Sixth Grade

Step 5: Final Victory ______
o Heard It All Before
o Fellowship & Worship
o Mostly Girls
o Media

Custom Curriculum Critique

Please take a moment to fill out this evaluation form, rip it out, fold it, tape it, and send it back to us. This will help us continue to customize products for you. Thanks!

1. Overall, please give this *Custom Curriculum* course (*N. T. Speedway)* a grade in terms of how well it worked for you. (A=excellent; B=above average; C=average; D=below average; F=failure) Circle one.

   A B C D F

2. Now assign a grade to each part of this curriculum that you used.

a. Upfront article	A	B	C	D	F	Didn't use
b. Publicity/Clip art	A	B	C	D	F	Didn't use
c. Repro Resource Sheets	A	B	C	D	F	Didn't use
d. Session 1	A	B	C	D	F	Didn't use
e. Session 2	A	B	C	D	F	Didn't use
f. Session 3	A	B	C	D	F	Didn't use
g. Session 4	A	B	C	D	F	Didn't use
h. Session 5	A	B	C	D	F	Didn't use

3. How helpful were the options?
   - ❑ Very helpful
   - ❑ Somewhat helpful
   - ❑ Not too helpful
   - ❑ Not at all helpful

4. Rate the amount of options:
   - ❑ Too many
   - ❑ About the right amount
   - ❑ Too few

5. Tell us how often you used each type of option (4=Always; 3=Sometimes; 2=Seldom; 1=Never)

	4	3	2	1
Extra Action	❑	❑	❑	❑
Combined Jr. High/High School	❑	❑	❑	❑
Urban	❑	❑	❑	❑
Small Group	❑	❑	❑	❑
Large Group	❑	❑	❑	❑
Extra Fun	❑	❑	❑	❑
Heard It All Before	❑	❑	❑	❑
Little Bible Background	❑	❑	❑	❑
Short Meeting Time	❑	❑	❑	❑
Fellowship and Worship	❑	❑	❑	❑
Mostly Guys	❑	❑	❑	❑
Mostly Girls	❑	❑	❑	❑
Media	❑	❑	❑	❑
Extra Challenge (High School only)	❑	❑	❑	❑
Sixth Grade (Jr. High only)	❑	❑	❑	❑

BUSINESS REPLY MAIL

FIRST CLASS MAIL PERMIT NO 1 ELGIN IL

POSTAGE WILL BE PAID BY ADDRESSEE

Attn: Youth Department

David C Cook Publishing Co
850 N GROVE AVE
ELGIN IL 60120-9980

NO POSTAGE NECESSARY IF MAILED IN THE UNITED STATES

(tape here)

6. What did you like best about this course?

7. What suggestions do you have for improving *Custom Curriculum*?

8. Other topics you'd like to see covered in this series:

9. Are you?
   - ❑ Full time paid youthworker
   - ❑ Part time paid youthworker
   - ❑ Volunteer youthworker

10. When did you use *Custom Curriculum*?
    - ❑ Sunday School
    - ❑ Small Group
    - ❑ Youth Group
    - ❑ Retreat
    - ❑ Other ______________________________

11. What grades did you use it with? ______________

12. How many kids used the curriculum in an average week? __________

13. What's the approximate attendance of your entire Sunday school program (Nursery through Adult)? __________

14. If you would like information on other *Custom Curriculum* courses, or other youth products from David C. Cook, please fill out the following:

Name: ______________________________
Church Name: ______________________________
Address: ______________________________
____
Phone: (____) ______________________________

Thank you!